AF447704

The Murder of Janette Roberson

Aria Benson

Published by Trellis Publishing, 2021.

While every precaution has been taken in the preparation of this book, the publisher assumes no responsibility for errors or omissions, or for damages resulting from the use of the information contained herein.

THE MURDER OF JANETTE ROBERSON

First edition. July 5, 2021.

Copyright © 2021 Aria Benson.

ISBN: 979-8224049370

Written by Aria Benson.

THE MURDER OF JANETTE ROBERSON

ARIA BENSON

One-third of murders in the United States turn into cold cases which means that the killers simply walk away without being punished. But with the advancements in the technology, the law enforcement has a new and powerful ally, and that is science. If a crime scene was properly processed in the past and the investigators collected all of the physical evidence, detectives can solve a murder even now, years or decades afterward. So police departments all over the States are closing cold cases rapidly and bringing justice to the families which are left behind.

Unfortunately, the murder of Janette Roberson still haunts Reed City, a small community in Michigan. A young mother was murdered in a very mysterious way while working - in the middle of the day. And no one heard a single thing. The murder itself is a real challenge since the killer disappeared without being noticed by anyone. The store was open and serving customers which is another peculiar detail. Surely, it was a busy day, but someone must have seen something because there is no such thing as the perfect murder.

The DNA technology could save this cold case, but the law enforcement is very secretive about the samples they have. Determining in which state they are is probably difficult because the crime scene wasn't analyzed well. But has been thirty-five years, and Janette Roberson's family still has no answers.

Early life

Janette Roberson was born on October 25th, 1955 in a small rural town in Georgia, USA. She was raised in very religious surroundings since the members of her family belonged to Jehovah's Witnesses. She also had one sister Lana, and the two of them were very close, never leaving each other's side when they were growing up. Janette was a gorgeous girl with long blonde hair and affectionate smile. She was very shy most of the time but knew how to communicate with people nevertheless. Everyone who met Janette only said positive things about her because she was caring and lovely. Of course, her future husband Alvin Roberson saw that in Janette right away and the two of them dated throughout high school, eventually marrying in their early twenties.

Being from a religious background, Janette valued her family a lot. Her parents did get a divorce and Janette's mother Marion Fisher moved to Reed City, Michigan to start her life over. She got a better job position working for the town's administration, and it was a huge opportunity for her. Janette started her own family with Alvin down in Georgia, but they decided to move to Michigan to be closer to Marion. They had two young kids and were ready to hit the road in spring of 1982. The Roberson family loved Reed City because the community itself was very small. Everyone knew everyone, and they accepted the newcomers quickly. Alvin found a job in a nearby town fixing cars while Janette stayed at home to take care of the kids.

The locals loved Janette and they recognized that she was a really good person. The family needed extra funds, so Janette decided to start looking for employment. She got a position of a salesperson at Gamble's hardware store. Janette was in charge of the pet store which was a perfect place for her. She enjoyed her work and took a great care of the little animals. Local kids would go in and spend hours playing at the pet store. Janette didn't mind, and she enjoyed the company. Things were looking alright for the Roberson's and they seemed to be happy with their new life. Unfortunately, at the beginning of January 1983, Janette heard a rumor that her husband was having an affair with a local woman and that might have shaken her up a little. But she continued to work, convinced it would help her stay focused.

The day of the murder

It was January 19th, 1983 and Reed City, Michigan was experiencing oddly warm weather. This pleased the workers at Gamble's hardware store and motivated them to continue their daily tasks because the new merchandise arrived on this day and they needed to bring everything inside, as well as to place the items on their shelves. Everyone was busy, carrying the boxes, so the store itself looked pretty deserted. However, customers were still going in and out, purchasing the groceries or other items they had on their shopping lists. Janette Roberson was in the store as well but she wasn't dealing with the trucks which were parked on both entrances to the shop. Instead, she was down in the basement, looking after the pet store part of the Gamble's. Her husband Alvin visited her at least twice that morning, and he also brought her lunch. He was still laid off from his job, so Alvin had plenty of free time.

One of their kids was sick and Janette took a break twice to check in on her. Carl Johnson arrived at the store to deliver gerbils to the pet store sometime between 10:00 AM and 11:00 AM. He entered the basement, looking for Janette but she was nowhere to be found. The man waited for about ten to fifteen minutes hoping that Janette would show up. He gave up and was informed by another clerk that Janette was probably out, tending to her kid at home. Janette was back at the shop at 11:30 AM and that was confirmed by a customer who saw her on the ground floor of the hardware store. He was browsing around, and Janette came up to him asking if he needed any help. He had never seen her before, so he guessed she was a new clerk. Jokingly he told Janette that he probably knew the store better than her since he shops there often.

It was very unusual to see Janette on the ground floor, but she probably went to the bathroom. The man asked Janette were is everyone, and she replied that they are outside, dealing with the delivery trucks. Janette excused herself and went down to the basement to her part of the hardware store. The man was probably the last person to see her alive. Then a woman went to the pet store section in order to find a chemical that would clean her fish tank. She noticed that the basement was empty and that there were no other customers around.

Also, there was no Janette. She went upstairs, asking where she is. The cashier from the ground floor told her that Janette was probably still on a break. The woman said she would come back later.

Sometime around 03:00 PM, two sisters Venus and Jan arrived with the intentions of buying fish food and other things for their large aquarium. They descended into the basement which was still deserted. The two of them continued with their business, picking up the things they needed, hoping that Janette would show up in the meantime. Noticing that they were still alone in the basement, they went upstairs and called the other cashier whose name was Angie. Angie went downstairs with them, used the bottom cash register and the sisters paid for the things they picked out. It is very likely that Janette was attacked during the time the two sisters were in the basement.

As they were going up to the ground floor, Venus and Jen observed that the hardware store was suddenly filled with customers. The manager showed up from the storage room and told Angie to go look for Janette. He pointed out that her coat was still on the hanger so she must be somewhere in the basement. Angie went straight to the backroom, assuming that Janette was there. The woman froze in the doorway because she saw Janette laying on the floor. She was covered in blood, and the entire scene looked highly disturbing. Angie gathered herself up and went to the ground floor. Still in shock, the woman told the manager that Janette is downstairs, pointing in the direction of the basement with a shaky hand. She was breathless, and it was obvious to everyone that something bad happened. One of the workers told the manager to call an ambulance because they thought Angie was having a heart attack.

The manager ran down the stairs to see what was going on. He returned in a couple of minutes announcing that the door should be locked and that no one should enter the hardware store. The manager ordered everyone to leave the basement area, and he contacted the authorities. The first responders entered the backroom, and they were shocked by the sight of Janette's body. She was attacked with multiple weapons in a very violent manner. The woman was also partially undressed which suggested that she was sexually assaulted. Her hair was sticky and bloody. Janette's sister Lana would later say: *"This was a brutal—very brutal –killing. I don't know how someone can do that to another person."* The ambulance was called in for a possible heart attack, and a nurse who was passing by the store saw the vehicle parked outside. She went into the store to see if she could help with anything. The nurse was led to the backroom and saw Janette's lifeless body. It was clear that she couldn't do a thing to help her now.

The investigation

Reed City was in a particular spot at the time, and there were three law enforcement agencies in charge of the area - the Reed City Police Department, the Michigan State Police, and the Osceola County Sheriff's Department. All three of them were notified of the murder, and they sent their officers and detectives to analyze the scene of the crime. Having in mind that Reed City had a small population, murder was not a common thing. Everyone assumed that three law enforcement agencies were more than enough to tackle this crime and find the culprit. It would later be determined that all three of them failed at sharing the information with each other.

Two officers Finkbeiner and Primeau from the Reed City Police Department arrived at 04:04 PM, exactly fourteen minutes after the discovery of Janette's body. The detective from the Osceola County Sheriff's Department arrived afterward. The scene of the crime was hectic, with customers and people walking around, talking, or waiting to be interviewed by the police. Instead of securing the basement, it seemed like the officers had no idea how to keep everyone away from the body. They sent Janette's corpse for an autopsy in order to determine the time of death. Finkbeiner and Primeau ordered that the entire basement should be dusted for prints to see who was in there on that day. They also suggested that all employees should be fingerprinted to make sure they could identify them easily.

The results of the autopsy showed that Janette was murdered sometime between 01:00 PM and 04:00 PM that day. It is a large timeframe which puzzled the investigators. Having in mind that she was murdered in the back room in the basement, it was strange how no one heard a thing. After all, you could make out people talking through the ceiling or floor, but no customer reported hearing screams or commotion in the basement. This led the investigators to assume that the murderer was someone Janette knew or they managed to shut her mouth in time so that she couldn't make a sound. Another odd thing was the fact that more than five people went into the basement during the time Janette was likely murdered. The police interviewed them, and it was confirmed that none of the customers saw anything which could be categorized as strange.

There was a possibility that the killer was in the back room the whole time, waiting for the right opportunity to escape. Everything pointed in the direction of a killer who knew Janette because the murder itself was very heated and personal. The person who did this used a variety of tools and weapons to attack Janette. It was clear that he was very angry at her. She was also sexually assaulted which confirmed the theory that the murder was done by someone who was in Janette's life at the moment. The police needed to dig deeper and find all connections Janette had with people in her surroundings. Perhaps the authorities could connect the dots and solve the murder quickly.

The law enforcement started interviewing the people who knew Janette. The Roberson's were still new in town, but they were making friends quickly. There were many friends and neighbors who wanted to help out and they were talking to the police. One of Janette's friends told the detectives that the woman told her about the alleged phone calls she received one day before the murder. Someone hang up the phone twice in one night, and Janette found it very odd. Not to forget that she did receive strange and disturbing phone calls in the past that started a few weeks after they moved to Reed City. Therefore, the detectives might be dealing with a stalker who watched Janette from afar. Perhaps he wanted more from her, and his behavior escalated. It is not uncommon for the murderers to stalk and frighten their victims prior to the killing itself.

Even though the possibility that a stranger murdered Janette, the police procedures suggest that the detectives should start from the family and expand outward. So they zeroed in on Janette's husband Alvin as their possible killer. Everyone knew that he was at the hardware store at least twice that morning and he was not working at the car shop. As a matter of fact, he had been at the family home for more than two weeks. Maybe Janette and Alvin got into a fight, and it became deadly? Or was it a quarrel gone bad? After all, Janette's body was so severely beaten that it was very possible someone was extremely angry at her. Also, the location of the crime scene shows that it was not premeditated because anyone could have walked in during the murder. It was a real mystery but every investigation has to start somewhere.

The suspects

As it was assumed, Alvin Roberson was the first person interviewed by the police. After all, he was Janette's husband and perhaps their marriage was not ideal. The law enforcement talked to Alvin's friends who worked with him at the car shop. They described Alvin as gentle and told the police how much the man cared about his family. It was unlikely that he would murder his wife. Alvin submitted his hair samples, as well as fingerprints and blood. It was the beginning of the 1980s so the DNA technology was not yet applied to catch the criminals. However, the police used the blood in order to test it for the blood type. It was the way to eliminate the suspects back then.

Alvin didn't have a solid alibi for the day of the murder. He was not working and was present at the crime scene at least a few times.

The detectives took his work clothes for analysis because they noticed red stains on his shoes. They looked like blood. It would later be determined that the stains were car paint. It had nothing to do with the killing. The crime scene analysis confirmed that Alvin's fingerprints were found in the basement, on the opposite side from the back room. As the time went by, the law enforcement was certain that Alvin didn't kill his wife. He did act strange days after the murder, but it can be justified because he was in grief and left with two young kids to take care of. He became a single father all of a sudden.

He clearly missed his wife, so no one was surprised when he started a relationship with their babysitter eight months after the murder. Some would say that the two were having an affair prior to Janette's murder and that the marriage was falling apart as a result. Alvin also stopped feeling comfortable in Reed City, and he decided to move back to Georgia. There was nothing for him in Michigan, so he packed up the bags and went south. After years and years of interviews, Alvin was publicly ruled out as a suspect.

Marion Fisher mentioned another possible suspect to the police. His name was Dave, and he lived in the same building as the Roberson family. Dave was a teenager who probably had a crush on Janette. He told one neighbor that he slept with Janette which was very likely untrue having in mind that Dave was still in high school and he was prone to lying. The law enforcement would probably ignore this boy completely, but he pretty much put the spotlight on himself. He printed a large wanted sign and placed it on his bedroom window. This occurred just a couple of days after the murder, so the police started asking around. Dave submitted his prints and blood for testing. Even though he spent a lot of time in the pet store where Janette worked, nobody has seen him on the day of the murder, and the chances are he was not present. The last time Dave was interviewed by the police was in 1985. He was not officially ruled out as a suspect, but it seems like the police are not able to connect Dave to the murder of Janette Roberson.

One month after the murder, the Reed City Police Department received an anonymous call that suggested they should take a closer look at Lee Peterson. He was a local army man who came back to Reed City in December of 1982. He suffered from mental illnesses which were confirmed by a nurse who worked at a foster house Peterson frequented. Peterson would focus on one of the nurses and then followed them around. He did fit the profile of a person who would stalk someone and make obscene telephone calls. He also lived in a nearby building when the murder occurred. He surely saw Janette Roberson somewhere around the town. But the thing that made the law enforcement interested in the possibility that Lee Peterson was the murderer is the fact that Peterson's mother was a previous owner of the hardware Janette worked at. Therefore, he knew the store and was capable of successfully hiding from the other shoppers and workers.

Lee Peterson's schizophrenia fit the crime itself because Janette was attacked with numerous weapons. However, even after several interviews with Peterson, the law enforcement haven't decided if they could connect him to the murder or not. We might never get to know more about him because Peterson committed suicide. His schizophrenia was getting worse and Peterson stopped taking his medications. Unable to fight the illness further, he took his own life. We do know that no one of the witnesses saw Peterson at the hardware store on the day of the murder of Janette Roberston. The chances are police took a closer look at him just because he was mentally ill and prone to violent outbursts.

The sketch

The investigation did hit a dead end because the police were out of possible suspects. Every lead they followed turned out fruitless. But they still had to identify every person that was seen in the hardware store on the day Janette Roberson was murdered. As previously mentioned, Reed City was a small community and people were close. They knew their neighbors and strangers were not common. The police managed to put a name to a face to almost every person that was at the scene of the crime but one man couldn't be identified. Flossie Earnest who worked at the hardware store remembered him and mentioned that an unknown man was at the store on that day in January. Flossie did see him before because he often shopped there in the weeks leading to the murder. But recalling his name was difficult.

Flossie worked with a sketch artist in order to produce a drawing of the man that was seen in the store. He was described as being in his twenties, with light hair, and wearing a blue jacket. Hoping that the public might help them with the identification, the police contacted *Osceola County Herald* and they published the sketch on February 3rd, 1983. The article that accompanied the sketch informed the public that the reward money is growing and that any information, no matter how minor it might seem could help the police find the murderer. Notable people from Reed City and surrounding towns were investing the money in the reward fund. Prosecutor James Talaske was one of them and he had this to say: *"This thing is really hanging over our town. It affects everyone. More people are buying guns. It's the little things that are happening that change the feeling of the whole community."*

A couple of days later, *Osceola County Herald* ran the story about the phone calls Janette received prior to the murder. Prosecutor James Talaske was once again asked to comment on this development, and he said: *"It's my understanding that the phone rang twice and the person on the other end hung up without saying anything. The calls could have been made in result of someone dialing the wrong number."*

On February 17th, 1983 the police did identify the man from the sketch. He was noticed while buying newspapers and the law enforcement was contacted. The man was driving a green car which was very rare, so they noticed him quickly. The officers took him into the custody and talked to the man for some time. In the end, they determined that the man had nothing to do with the murder and that he was simply shopping in the hardware store. The mysterious man was released, and it was announced that the man was no longer a suspect in this case.

The aftermath

The police had nowhere to go with this case, and it slowly became cold. They even accepted the help of a psychic reader hoping she would provide them with some hints that would lead to capturing the killer. Unfortunately, they had nothing to go on. The people living in Reed City, Michigan refused to let go of this case, and they have been making annual walks through the town on the day of the murder in order to remind everyone that this case is still unsolved and that the law enforcement should do something about it. They call it *Justice for Janette,* and it keeps the memory of this lovely woman alive.

Janette Roberson's family is very vocal and they are pleading for her murder to be solved. It has been thirty-five years, and there are still no answers. Lana Jarvie, Janette's sister is one of the leaders of *Justice for Janette,* and she is sure that the police dropped the ball when they failed to secure the crime scene properly. Lana is certain that plenty of useful evidence might have been lost in the process. She also claims that the detectives shouldn't have focused on Janette's husband so hard because they might have overlooked other suspects. Lana says: *"There is a murderer walking around free. Somebody has to know something, had to have seen something that day. Maybe it is something small, something they think is irrelevant – it's not."*

Janette's mother Marion died before the case was solved which was another tragic blow to the family. But it is comforting to see that a large number of Reed City residents support *Justice for Janette.* Mary Beth Beemer, who lives in this town said the following: *"This is a small community. We have to have faith the murderer is found. It's also important for the annual walk, to let everyone know that this isn't finished — that we aren't finished until we find out. This has not ended."* Hopefully, the police would break this case soon because Janette and her family deserve justice.

THE MURDER OF IRA YARMOLENKO

DANIELLE SWEET

On a seemingly normal Thursday afternoon on the Catawba River in May of 2008, two jet skiers planned on having a picnic together along the river when they stumbled upon a peculiar sight that would change their lives forever - a car crashed into a stump on the banks of the river along with the horrifying sight of a dead body lying next to it. They quickly alerted authorities and soon discovered that the body was that of a deceased young woman.

This was the tragic fate of Irina "Ira" Yarmolenko, a University of North Carolina college student who had just celebrated her twentieth birthday several days earlier. She was discovered with three items from her car tied around her neck. There was no sign of a struggle or any clear indication of a motive. She was not sexually assaulted or robbed.

Although first responders initially thought her death could have been a suicide, her death was ruled a homicide by asphyxiation. To this day, her murder still garners interest from the public due to the strange yet disturbing circumstances surrounding her death. Add to that the whispers that surround the case about the possibility that her convicted murderer, Mark Carver, might actually be an innocent man. What followed this horrific discovery was an investigation into the crime scene and into her personal life to uncover what happened to Ira.

Ira's early life and college experience

Ira Yarmolenko was born in the Ukraine on May 2nd, 1988 but emigrated to the United States when she was eight, along with her parents and brother Pavel. The family reportedly fled the Ukraine as refugees due to religious persecution. Her parents, both research scientists, were able to find job opportunities in North Carolina.

Ira quickly picked up the language and by all accounts seemed to assimilate well into American culture. She lived in North Carolina for most of her life, spoke with a southern accent and had several personal interests. Like most teenagers, she enjoyed hiking, acting, photography, sports, and music.

She also played the piano and liked listening to bands, such as the Counting Crows. She was also extremely academic. She excelled in math and science while being an active member of her high school poetry team. Ira was especially close to her family. Although she left Chapel Hill for UNC Charlotte, about a 3-hour drive away, she spoke to her mother almost every day. After her death, her mother said to reporters, "I don't think what I'm living is called life anymore."

During her two years in college, she found other interests beyond her required coursework at UNC Charlotte, where she was an undeclared major but had a strong interest in French. She was a photographer for the University Times, her college paper, and occasionally wrote columns and articles for the Niner Online, an online student-run newspaper.

She was also a member of the university's Russian Club as Russian was her first language. Her Russian language classmate described her as, "the kind of girl that always made you feel special, wanted, needed, cared for, and loved. It always seemed like she was always so happy to see you, and would always take at least a second of her time to say hello to you." It was here that she met her roommate Masha, another student from the Ukraine.

Masha and Ira bonded over the fact that they both spoke Russian and came from similar backgrounds. Masha described the day that she found out Ira was murdered when two investigators showed up at the small apartment that she shared with Ira, "It was her student I.D. picture. And I just started screaming. Sorry. Both of our families immigrated here to this country for a better life and sacrificed so much." Like most people close to Ira, Masha was devastated to hear the news of her friend's death.

Most people who knew Ira described her as outgoing. They felt that she would not have been afraid if a stranger had approached her. She was involved on campus and worked at a local coffee shop, Jackson's Java. Years after her death, her picture could still be found on the counter of Jackson's Java. She had a lasting impact on those that knew her. Her brother said, "Everything that she's ever done was to help people."

At UNC Charlotte, she had many close friends and acquaintances who described her as a cheerful and bubbly person, yet still high-achieving. In addition to her job at the coffee shop, Ira also worked as an aid in a computer lab on campus. The week before finals, her roommate Masha and friends threw a party for her 20th birthday.

During this party, her friends reported that Ira ended up cooking for everyone there, despite the fact that party was a celebration in her honor. This was not uncommon for her to do and was just the kind of person she was. Her friends concluded the celebration by visiting an art exhibit. They reported that she was in good spirits and that they parted amicably.

Although it seemed Ira was thriving in her environment at UNC Charlotte, she was in the process of closing her chapter there and beginning a new one at UNC-Chapel Hill, a school a bit closer to home. "Ira indicated she was sad to leave her friends behind at UNCC, but she was looking forward to attending UNC-Chapel Hill in the fall," according to Sgt. Tindall, an investigator in the case.

She had resigned from her positions at the coffee shop and in the computer lab where she had worked during her sophomore year shortly before she was murdered. Her brother Pavel, a then Ph.D. graduate student at Duke said, "She was not sure how she felt about leaving Charlotte. But she was very, very excited about coming to Chapel Hill."

Ira intended on transferring to UNC-Chapel Hill to be closer to her family and to major in public health. The day of her murder, she visited the coffee shop and said goodbye to her friends there and left a gift, a book, for her former boss. She also took several items to the Goodwill to donate and visited her credit union where she deposited some checks before heading to the river about 20 miles away.

The scene of the crime

The Catawba River is over 200 miles long and spans two states. It is located about 20 minutes from Charlotte and is popular among fisherman, boaters and jet skiers. First responders on that fateful day described a perplexing, yet disturbing scene.

The doors on the driver's side of Ira's car were opened, and her body was found just a few feet away. It did not appear she was sexually assaulted or robbed, nor did she have defensive wounds from fighting off her attacker or attackers.

Three ligatures were found around her neck: a nylon ribbon from a bag in her car, a drawstring from the hood of a jacket and a bungee cord. The drawstring was wrapped around her neck. The ribbon was wrapped once around her neck and oddly tied in a bow in the front. Her hair and body were also wet, although she was found on dry ground.

According to Detective Terry during the trial, "Her head was back towards the embankment. Her feet were near the river underneath some brush. Upon closer inspection, she was actually holding some of that brush in her hand. . . ." It was determined that this was the place where she was murdered and that she had not been transferred there.

Investigators began piecing together her movements before arriving at the river banks and determined it was likely that she headed down to the river banks to take pictures, as she was an avid photographer. Her brother Pavel said he "wasn't surprised she would go to such a remote spot. She was adventurous. She once hiked the Stampede Trail in Alaska with friends, searching for an abandoned bus made famous by Jon Krakauer's book Into the Wild."

Her camera was found in the trunk of her car, but there was not any film in it that could yield any clues about her death. Investigators quickly began interviewing people along the river to see if anyone had heard or seen anything out of the ordinary and came across two fishermen who were fishing about 100 yards from where Ira's body and car were discovered.

Mark Carver and Neil Cassada were cousins who grew up in the area and had been fishing in a new spot they had discovered the weekend before. This spot was about 100 yards from where Ira's car and body were discovered. Carver had been excited about the spot. He had returned to it because it did not require him to haul his boat to the river which was difficult for Carver to do since he suffers from carpal tunnel syndrome, a condition that makes his hands extremely weak.

His doctors recommended he not lift anything heavier than five pounds. Cassada also suffered from a heart condition, making it difficult to do anything too physical. Investigators questioned both men who reported that they had not seen Ira or had not heard anything from their fishing spot. They did report hearing a scraping sound that sounded like noise from construction.

They both willingly provided their DNA to investigators and went on their way. With the lack of forensic clues pointing toward any viable suspects, it was not until forensic analysis of the car several months later revealed partial DNA matches for Carver and Cassada that they became the prime suspects for Ira's murder. Mark Carver and Neal Cassada were arrested in December of 2008, seven months after her death and charged with conspiracy and murder. A day before Cassada's the trial began in 2010, Cassada died of a heart attack. Carver has always proclaimed their innocence.

"Simple" life of Mark Carver

Simple is the word often used to describe Mark Carver. "Simple in his routine, simple in his thought process, simple in his desires and wants," defense attorney Brent Ratchford said to reporters. Unlike Ira, Carver is not well-educated and has limitations with writing and reading comprehension, which he has struggled with throughout most of his life.

At an early age, he was placed in special education classes because of these limitations and his relatively low IQ. At 16, he dropped out of school to work in a mill. At the time he was arrested, it was documented that he was taking medication prescribed for schizophrenia.

Carver is also the father of four children from two different marriages. "He lived for his children and family," his sister-in-law Robin Carver said when asked about him. "He didn't really do much of anything else. Fishing and hunting and family, that was about it."

Although his family speaks well of Carver, like most family members often do, he did have prior brushes with the law despite never being convicted of a crime. In 2005, Carver faced a charge of injury to property. Carver purportedly confronted two people he thought were stealing his four-wheeler. The charge was dismissed, and the file no longer exists. A year before Ira's murder, Carver accidentally shot his son. Carver and his son were supposedly wrestling when the gun went off. "It was an accident," his son said. The case was later dismissed and Carver never convicted of a crime.

Cassada also had had his own dealings with the law. In 1995, he was accused of assault and injury to personal property. He reportedly pointed a gun at someone. But the charges were dismissed and the details remain unclear.

His family insists that he had nothing to do with Ira's murder and that the stress of the trial for a crime he did not commit ultimately led to his death. Kaye Cassada, Neal Cassada's wife said "After 37 years of loving that man and being married to that man, I know he is not capable of hurting anybody. He would have died to help somebody." Charges against Cassada were dropped, a common proceeding with deceased suspects. His family attended the hearing and his son Shannon Cassada said, "We want everybody to hear that he was an innocent man."

Carver also maintains his own innocence, stating "they said that they had ... my DNA and Neal's DNA in the car. I know that's a lie because Neal left, and they couldn't have gotten no DNA because I wasn't down there. I didn't go around it. I didn't go around the car. You know what I'm saying?" He also said he didn't think Cassada would commit such a crime because "He's got four young'uns himself."

Although lie detector tests are not reliable enough to be used in court, during the initial investigation Cassada took a polygraph test, which he passed. Because he passed, investigators did not give Carver one. Carver has been very vocal about his willingness to also take a polygraph test.

Touch DNA

During the investigation and trial, Carver never wavered in proclaiming his innocence and said this to Ira's family "I never seen her that day. If I'd knowed she was up there, I would have went up there and helped her. They could have easily come down and killed me just like they did her."

His trial began in 2010. Before the trial, Carver was offered a surprising plea deal from the prosecution: 4-8 years in prison if he pleaded guilty to second degree murder. Had he taken this deal and pled guilty to murder he could be out of prison and with his family. His attorney said, "I have never gotten such a low offer. And to me that spoke volumes about the case." Carver turned down this offer and prosecutors moved forward with the case.

Prosecutors argued that the two men killed Ira because she witnessed or photographed something they did not want her to see. As a result, they strangled her and pushed her car on the embankment where their DNA was transferred to the car. Their intention was to sink the car in the water, but it hit a stump where it stayed until it was finally discovered by the jet skiers. They then returned to their fishing spot until they were questioned by police.

Prosecutors relied on a relatively new forensic technique at the time known as "touch DNA." Unlike previous methods, touch DNA uses smaller amounts of DNA, such as skin cells transferred to a person or object when they come into contact with someone. But touch DNA is not as reliable as other DNA methods requiring blood or saliva because it is difficult to determine the origin of these cells. For instance, skin cells can be transferred indirectly by a third party or carrier.

For example, a man in California was falsely imprisoned because his DNA was found on a murder victim. It was determined that it was impossible that he was a killer because he had a solid alibi. At the time of the murder, he was unconscious in a hospital due to extreme intoxication.

Prosecutors then discovered that the same paramedic who treated him for intoxication was a first responder at the murder scene. The DNA from the intoxicated man was presumably transferred to the victim by the paramedic. This case set a precedent about the reliability of touch DNA and is cited by Carver's advocates for innocence as a possibility as to why Carver's and Cassada's DNA was found on Ira's car.

Despite this interesting theory, it was not presented by the defense in Carver's trial and the jury found him guilty of murder. He was sentenced to and is currently serving life in prison. Carver's advocates argue that the car and crime scene was not preserved, and that Carver and Cassada's DNA could have been transferred by officers or other people near the crime scene. Many officers, the jet skiers, first responders were all present at the crime scene and could have all inadvertently transferred the DNA to the car.

Several other inconsistencies exist in the prosecution's case. Carvers DNA was not found on her body nor on the trunk of the car where he and Cassada would have pushed it into the river bank according to prosecutors. Carvers DNA did not match a third DNA profile found on the bungee cord and the only DNA found under Ira's fingernails was her own.

His attorney and advocates also argue that the two men couldn't have physically pushed the car into the river bank due to Carver's carpal tunnel and Cassada's heart condition. Cassada supposedly got winded just walking. In 2013, Carver's attorneys filed an appeal on his behalf, but the appeals court determined "no error in the defendant's trial" occurred, meaning his conviction of life in prison would be upheld. But this did not deter his advocates from trying to prove Carver did not receive a fair defense during his trial.

Earlier this year, a judge granted the request of the North Carolina Actual Innocence Project, attorneys who have become interested in Carver case who believe Carver is wrongfully imprisoned, to see DNA reports that were never shared with Carvers defense team, along with further DNA testing.

They argue that Carver did not receive a proper defense as his lawyers did not call any witnesses or DNA experts to the stand and address the DNA evidence, and that the DNA evidence is not compelling enough beyond a reasonable doubt to warrant a life sentence for Carver. It is the only evidence linking Carver to the crime. Only time will determine the final outcomes of Carver's appeals as the evidentiary hearing has been postponed. Legal proceedings could take several years.

Other suspects

If Carver and Cassada's DNA was indeed transferred by a third party and they did not kill Ira, then who did? There was no one in her life that seemed to have any motive. Besides these two men, there was only one other suspect in her murder investigation. Nine months after the murder, Christopher Lemont Cooper wrote a letter to News anchor Erica Bryant to "confess a sin," that he and several other accomplices had killed Ira.

He said he drove a van full of friends that were all high and needed money for drugs. He said he was unable to sleep "because of what we did to that young woman." And wished to meet with the reporter. The TV station did not publish the letter and turned it over to investigators where they took the letter very seriously and launched an investigation with the North Carolina State Bureau of Investigations.

Police and investigators visited Cooper, where he was in jail on charges of rape, assault by strangulation, and for being delinquent in child support. He reportedly refused to cooperate with investigators, but they ultimately ruled him out as a suspect concluding that several of the accomplices he named were incarcerated at the time of the murder. They also cleared the other accomplices named in Cooper's letter and continued building their case against Carver and Cassada.

Free Mark Carver

Free Mark Carver is one of the prominent websites advocating for the release of Carver. They believe he is innocent or at the very least did not receive a proper defense in his trial. The website is run by a former newspaper journalist who now works in the fashion industry. She had no ties to the case or families and became intrigued with the case in 2011 after its details aired on Dateline NBC and through other online news articles.

One of the major theories from Carver's advocates presented on the website is that Ira was not murdered and in fact committed suicide by placing the ligatures around her neck herself. They claim that Ira was not the cheerful person described by her friends and loved ones and that she had battled depression.

Her boyfriend had broken up with her shortly before her murder and her poetry was sometimes dark and melancholy. The website alludes to accounts from unnamed people who claim that Ira had attempted suicide when she was younger and had seen a therapist at UNC Charlotte. The website does not provide sources and only mentions them as letters to the author.

Although this theory may be offensive to those who loved Ira and describe her as a happy and vibrant young woman, it has been addressed by pathologists who have dismissed this theory saying "For this to have been anything but a homicide, i.e., this was a suicide, this victim would have to tie three ligatures around her neck tightly and before death get into this position while that's going on and her legs underneath the brush given that position and I just feel like that was not consistent with what we are seeing. . . . Yes, and another thing that this illustrates a little bit better also is the presence of particular matter, soil and grass on her skirt as well. So that's another thing that would have had to happen. If this was a suicide she would have had to do all this stuff by herself. It is just not consistent with that theory."

Her brother Pavel, who has since completed his Ph.D. in biomedical engineering and continues to conduct research at a pediatric hospital, said he has read some of the internet theories about his sister's death, but they are "not grounded in reality." He asserts that his sister never attempted suicide and there was no indication she was depressed. Nevertheless, the fact remains that a lively, young woman lost her life just days after her 20th birthday.

Memorials

We may never know what really happened to Ira or why someone chose to take her life but it is clear that she touched many people who strive to keep her memory alive. The jet skiers who found her body, Dennis Lovelace and Brenda Pierce, placed a memorial cross where they found her car. The changing levels of the Catawba river sometimes covers part of the cross, but it is still visible to visitors.

A memorial bench as far as Alaska, where Ira spent a summer waitressing, also bears her name. "A Kansas City based artist Shane Blindt designed and installed this bench at the request of many co-workers whose lives were touched with Ira's presence during the 2007 McKinley Village Lodge summer season. Lettering on the memorial was hand drawn with pen showing the elegance and beauty of Ira's outward expressions contrasted with a raw and rugged placement into the world she left behind." It is maintained by locals there.

Her high school poetry team in Chapel Hill renamed the group The Sacrificial Poets in her honor.

What Time Devours is a book written by her former professor at UNC Charlotte who dedicated his book to her memory. He directed a campus production, which Ira was a part of the previous year before she was murdered. He also included a line from her poetry and her picture in the dedication of the book.

The controversy around her murder continues to intrigue people and several websites and pages are dedicated to outlining the details of the case. Ira's murder has been featured on Dateline and 20/20. She continues to captivate an almost cult following, and many people are still tirelessly working to prove that Carver is innocent and did not receive a fair trial. If this is the case, it means that justice has not been served for Ira and her family. But one thing is for sure, the memory of Ira Yarmolenko will continue to live on with her family, friends, and strangers that have been touched by her story.

THE MURDER OF MICHELE MACNEILL

KATE LEONARD

On the surface, the MacNeill family seemed perfect. Martin, a successful physician, and his wife Michele, lived in a gated community in Utah's Pleasant Grove neighborhood. The couple had four biological children, and had adopted four more. They were well-liked, and were all active in the Church of Latter Day Saints. Behind closed doors, though, a storm was brewing that was about to turn deadly.

Martin MacNeill was born on February 1st, 1956, in New Jersey. The MacNeills were a very poor family. After his parents' divorce Martin claims his mother went into prostitution, and raised him and his siblings in a one bedroom apartment. He also claimed that he and his siblings all suffered horrendous abuse in their childhoods. As they grew older, most of Martin's siblings turned to drugs and alcohol to cope with their trauma. One of his sisters, and one of his brothers ended up committing suicide, and all but one of the others died of addiction-related illnesses.

Martin joined the military at just 17 by lying about his age. Two years later he was diagnosed as a "latent schizophrenic" after telling doctors he was hearing voices. He was given disability leave, and received both Veteran's benefits, and Social Security benefits for years. It is not known for certain whether Martin's diagnosis was correct, or whether he only joined the military in order to scam the government out of benefits.

Shanna Hogan, a writer who penned a comprehensive book on the case called *The Stranger She Loved*, notes that most of Martin's life involved control, manipulation, and fairly meticulous long-term planning, which are not characteristic of a schizophrenic. She describes him as a "textbook sociopath."

Soon after receiving his leave from the military, Martin moved to California and decided to get involved with the Mormon church. He met his future wife, Michele, at a Latter Day Saint's event for community youth.

Michele Marie Somers was born on January 15th, 1957 in Concord, California. She was popular with her peers, a good student, a cheerleader, and an active member of the church. Michele was also a notable beauty; she won homecoming queen, and Miss Concord in 1976.

Michele's family did not approve of her dating Martin. Her mother and sister both remembered having bad feelings about him. He was arrogant and self-righteous, and made no attempt to ingratiate himself to the family. Linda Cluff, Michele's sister, later said, "He just gave me the creeps." Michele and Martin decided to date in secret to avoid her family's scrutiny.

Martin was emotionally manipulative from the very beginning of their relationship. He would often threaten suicide if Michele was angry at him, or of she expressed interest in ending the relationship. He began to isolate Michele from her family, saying she shouldn't be around them if they disapproved of their relationship.

Despite their troubles, the couple decided to get married. They eloped on February 21st, 1978. A few months later, Martin's history of deception began to come to light. He was arrested for cashing $35,000 of fake cheques, and using the money to buy jewelry, furniture, appliances, and clothes. Martin said he was inspired to begin the crime spree after watching a *60 Minutes* episode on how cheque forgery works. He bragged to friends that he would be able to pull off the scam better and more simply than the people in the news program. The fraud caught up with him, though, and just 4 months after he married Michele, Martin spent six months in jail for forgery.

When Martin was released from prison the couple began to expand their family, and moved around a lot. They lived in Mexico in 1980 while Martin attended a semester of medical school in Guadalajara. They then lived briefly in California and New York. By the time Martin obtained his medical licence in 1987, the MacNeills had four children, and were living in Utah.

It was later discovered that Martin was in possession of a seal and some stationary from St. Martin's University, where he did his undergraduate degree. He had falsified his transcripts in order to get into medical school. He did the same thing when transferring from his medical school in Mexico to one in California. He claimed he received several credits through a military program that he did not actually complete.

During this time he was also still lying to the military and Social Services. He said he was not working, and not attending school, which made him eligible for 100% benefits from both institutions.

Martin began working at the Brigham Young University Health Center, in Utah, while earning a law degree from the school. He graduated BYU in 1990. Martin and Michele's biological children were older, and had moved out of the house to attend various colleges. The MacNeills decided to adopt four more children from the Ukraine. One of the adopted children, though, did not fit in with the family. The MacNeills put her into foster care, and nullified the adoption.

Later that year, another girl in foster care, Sabrina, came to visit one of the MacNeills' adopted daughters. She herself had been given up by her adopted family, after they decided they only wanted to keep her younger sister. The MacNeills decided to adopt Sabrina.

They now had eight children: their biological children Rachel, Vanessa, Alexis, and Damian, and their adopted children Giselle, Sabrina, Elle, and Ada. It was later revealed that the youngest child, Ada, was actually Vanessa's daughter that Martin and Michele were raising as their own.

Giselle said they adopted kids weren't treated well by Martin. She said, "I was more of a slave girl", in charge of cooking, cleaning, and general upkeep of the household. She also recalled an incident in which Martin began touching her inappropriately while the family watched TV. Overall his daughters described him as, "haughty, stern, and arrogant."

Martin continued the emotional abuse of his wife, and his threats of suicide, and even graduated to physical threats. Several times Michele had caught Martin watching pornography, an act which she personally disliked, but was also not allowed in the Mormon church. During one such confrontation in August 2000, Martin threatened Michele with a butcher knife. Their son Damian managed to get the knife away from his father, and protect his mother. The police were called to the home, and Martin spent the night in a mental health facility.

Michele strongly suspected that Martin was having affairs with multiple women. She confided in her daughter Alexis, and asked her to help prove he was cheating. Alexis got ahold of her father's phone by telling him she was going to download a ringtone for him. She then retrieved his passcode, and used it to look up his phone records.

Alexis and Michele noticed that Martin had a lot of contact with one particular number. They paid a service to find out who the number belonged to. The woman was Gypsy Willis, a nurse Martin had met and begun an affair with in late 2005. Any confrontation about his involvement with other women would be met with anger. Martin never admitted to an affair to his wife.

In 2007 the family was doing well financially. They lived in the Pleasant Grove neighborhood of Utah, in a gated community. Martin began pushing Michele to get plastic surgery. She told him she wanted to lose weight, and lower her blood pressure before considering surgery, but he insisted she go ahead with the procedure. Michele believed that a facelift might make her more attractive to Martin, which may stop his affairs, and fix their marriage. She agreed to a consultation with a doctor of Martin's choosing.

Martin chose Dr. Scott Thompson to do his wife's surgery. He gave the doctor a list of drugs he wanted prescribed to her, including Lortab, Ambien, Valium, Percocet, Phenergan, and Keflex. Dr. Thompson agreed to prescribe the medication, as Martin was a certified physician, and he assumed Martin would be overseeing the administration of the drugs to ensure Michele's safety. He did note, though, that this was an unprecedented prescription for him. Dr. Thompson said he "never prescribed the combination of drugs listed above to a patient and would not have in this case had it not been for the recommendation of Martin MacNeill, and then only on the condition that Mr. MacNeill monitor the administration of the substances as a physician."

On April 3rd, 2007, Michele MacNeill underwent a routine facelift operation. She spent the night in the hospital and returned home the next day, where her daughter Alexis was spending time on break from medical school. On April 5th, Alexis found her mother "listless and unresponsive" in her bed. She confronted her father about the doses of medication he was giving to her mother. Martin told Alexis he "probably over-medicated" Michele, but that her mother would be fine.

Michele didn't believe the large doses of medication were an accident. They were making her feel drowsy, and nauseated to the point of vomiting. She insisted she didn't need anything for pain, but Martin gave her the drugs anyway. Alexis took over her mother's care to attempt to protect her from Martin.

Michele told her daughter of her fears that Martin had nefarious motives for over-medicating her. She told Alexis, "If anything happens to me, make sure it was not your dad." On April 10th, Alexis had to leave Utah to return to school.

On April 11th, 2007, Michele MacNeill died. When she got the call, Alexis suspected her father immediately. She said, "I just had this overwhelming feeling that he had done it."

Martin had several different accounts of what happened to his wife that day. In some tellings he said she was unconscious and underwater in the bath, in others he said she was slumped over the bath, hanging off the side of the tub. The incongruity in his stories wasn't the only suspicious happening that day.

That morning, Martin had attended the safety fair at the Utah State Developmental Center where he was working as their clinical director. According to a co-worker, he was extremely agitated, and "very insistent" he get his picture taken at the fair "so that people would know he was present." Martin continued to be aggressive toward his co-workers throughout the fair, and even ended up having a complaint filed against him.

At some point during the morning, Martin called his wife and left a voicemail feigning concern for her wellbeing. He said, "Michele, don't you dare, don't you go anywhere. Don't you go anywhere. Take it easy. Please, I'm very concerned. You just stay where you're at. I'm coming home. I'm going to make you a sandwich and we'll have a lovely lunch together, but just don't call anybody and don't go anywhere."

Investigators believe this was Martin's way of giving himself an alibi for the time of Michele's death, and of attempting to make himself look like a loving, attentive husband.

After the safety fair that morning, Martin said he picked up 6-year-old Ada from school, and drove her home, where he alone found the body of his wife. He said he left Ada in the car, then asked her to go get help when he found Michele. Ada, however, told the Children's Justice Center that she went into the house with Martin, and also saw Michele in the bath.

Martin called 911, and was exceedingly belligerent to the dispatcher. He hung up on her three times, and never spoke clearly enough for her to get a definitive address. Martin told the dispatcher that he was doing CPR on Michele, but when neighbors came to help, she was still in the tub, and would not have been in the position to receive chest compressions.

After Martin's calls with the 911 dispatcher, Doug Daniels, a neighbor of the MacNeills, came to help Martin get Michele out of the tub and attempt to revive her. Martin was apparently too weak to do this himself.

Investigators believe Martin began lying to his community months prior about having a disease so he would have an excuse for his inability to pull Michele from the tub on his own. He had claimed to several members of the LDS Church that he had cancer, and would occasionally walk with a cane to keep up the illusion of illness.

Doug and Martin began doing CPR on Michele. Doug was in charge of the chest compressions, while Martin knelt at her head and performed the CPR breaths.

Doug noticed Michele had a significant amount of mucous on her mouth and nose which would, in his estimation, make the procedure much more difficult. He looked around the bathroom for towels to wipe it away, but there weren't any. He noticed that none of the mucous transferred to Martin's face while he was allegedly giving her CPR. Doug also does not recall seeing Michele's chest rise and fall during Martin's breaths. Looking back, it seemed to Doug that Martin was only pretending to revive his wife.

Doug said he went to the laundry room after Michele had been taken to the hospital. There he found a pile of the missing towels. They were wet and had blood on them. Since he arrived before Michele was taken from the bath, and Martin had not left the scene since, the towels had to have been taken from the bathroom before he arrived on the scene.

In an affidavit, investigator Doug Witney said of Daniels' testimony, "This would indicate that Martin MacNeill would have to have stopped any lifesaving measure long enough to wipe up blood and water on the floor. The only other alternative to this inconsistency is that there was another person in the home during this time, assisting MacNeill". Michele's daughter Alexis believes her father's mistress, Gypsy, had a hand in her mother's death and may have been in the house as well.

Martin began acting very suspiciously immediately after Michele's death. He began collecting her things and putting them out into the garage. He also nonchalantly showed visitors around the house, pointing out the newest renovations they had done. He didn't seem at all distraught at the death of his wife.

Martin instructed his son Damian to dispose of Michele's medications so nobody would see them. He said he didn't want people knowing about Michele's plastic surgery for privacy reasons. Of course her medication should have been given to both the medical professionals and the police so they could properly determine the cause and manner of her death. As a physician Martin would have known the importance of disclosing Michele's medical history to those attempting to figure out what happened to her.

Alexis was also aware of the importance of telling investigators what medication her mother was on. When she asked her father where the medication was, he said the police must have already taken it.

Despite their avid protests, Martin was insistent on bringing his two oldest daughters, Rachel and Alexis, into the bathroom where Michele had died, showing them how he had tried to help their mother, and describing to them exactly what had happened. He kept saying they needed to get an autopsy done as soon as possible, because he was worried that people would believe he had killed her.

Despite Martin's strange behavior, and the misgivings of Michele's friends and family, the police concluded her death was accidental. One report stated, "The victim had apparently slipped and fell after filling the tub with water". Another officer's report backed this up; it read, "It appeared the female was drawing a bath when she possibly passed out or fell."

The autopsy also concluded Michele died of cardiovascular disease. Her death was recorded as due to accidental and natural causes.

Michele's funeral was on April 14th, 2007. Martin ensured none of Michele's family, except for her younger sister, was allowed to attend the service. Martin threatened to call the police on them if they should show up. They agreed with the rest of the family that Martin probably had something to do with Michele's death.

Martin spoke at the funeral, but barely mentioned Michele. He used the platform to complain about how unfair his life had been. He called his family "the definition of dysfunctional" and told stories about his brother Roy's suicide. The guests were all unnerved by Martin's seeming lack of interest in remembering his wife.

At the post-service luncheon Martin seemed actually happy. He was social, outgoing, and was even making jokes about how he was now a single man. Alexis approached her father and said she would gladly move in and be a nanny to the younger children if he needed her. He told her he had already hired someone.

Martin's odd behavior continued after the funeral. He returned to work on the Monday after the weekend service. His co-workers told him he didn't need to be there, but he just said he had nothing to do at home and continued with his work. They also noticed he was wearing a different wedding ring. He said he had lost his original ring, but didn't feel comfortable without one, so he bought a new one.

Three days after the funeral, despite having told Alexis it was already taken care of, Martin told Rachel that he was looking for a nanny for the younger children. She didn't think it was necessary, but still went to the temple with her father to pray for guidance on the issue. Outside the temple an odd performance ensued. A woman came up to Martin and Rachel and introduced herself to them as though they were meeting for the first time. Rachel remembers it was a strange encounter. She said, "The whole thing had been scripted."

The woman was Gypsy Willis, who Martin had been dating for over a year. Martin told Alexis over the phone about the family's new nanny. He also pretended to her that the two had just met. Alexis told her father she knew Gypsy, as Michele had been certain she was one of the women Martin was having an affair with. Martin got angry at Alexis and told the rest of his family not to speak to her again.

A few weeks later, Gypsy Willis moved into the MacNeill home. The children were told she was their new nanny, but they don't recall her doing any housework, or cooking for them. She either kept to herself in her basement bedroom, or was out with Martin. When Rachel and Alexis brought this fact up to their father, the two were forcibly removed from the house.

Martin and Gypsy began identity fraud in order to create a new persona for Gypsy. They applied for fake driver's licences and opened bank accounts under assumed names. The most personal and outrageous of all their crimes came when they stole Martin's adopted daughter's identity.

In July 2007, Giselle MacNeill was sent back to the Ukraine to visit her biological sister. Martin had no intention of letting her return to the family. Martin and Gypsy used Giselle's identity to set up more false identification documents for Gypsy. Gypsy Willis became Jillian Giselle MacNeill. The couple obtained a marriage licence, using the date of Michele's funeral as their false wedding date. The couple never officially married.

The crimes eventually caught up with Martin and Gypsy. In January of 2009, Martin was indicted on nine counts of aiding and abetting aggravated identity theft, making false statements, and misuse of a Social Security number.

He pleaded guilty to two of the aiding and abetting charges, and was sentenced to four years in prison. Gypsy was indicted on eleven counts of aggravated identity theft, and misuse of Social Security numbers. She was sentenced to 21 months in prison. In September 2009 Martin pleaded guilty to additional, federal charges of false and inconsistent statements, insurance fraud, and forgery. He received an additional 3 years in prison.

On January 16th, 2010, while Martin was in prison, his son Damian committed suicide. Damian was the only MacNeill sibling who didn't believe Martin killed Michele. In a letter to the press he wrote, "Some people are quick to infer that because of my father's actions following my mother's death, he had to also be involved somehow in the death itself. This seems ludicrous to me." Alexis had the opposite feeling about her brother's death. She said, "No matter what, my dad was involved; even if it was a suicide".

Michele's family could not shake the feeling that Martin had something to do with her death. They pushed for a re-examination of her autopsy and the circumstances surrounding her death. In October 2010, medical examiner Dr. Todd Grey reassessed the autopsy report. He found enough evidence to add drug toxicity to the cause of death. He also concluded that Michele could not have administered the drugs to herself.

By the time Martin was released from prison, on July 6th, 2012, an investigation was already underway to prove whether or not he had a hand in his wife's death. On August 24th, 2012, the Utah County Attorney's Office charged Martin with the murder of his wife.

The trial began on October 17th, 2013. Several women began to come forward and say they had had affairs with Martin. One of these women, Anna Osborne Walthall, told of some disturbing "pillow talk" the two allegedly shared. She said Martin had told her of a way to induce a heart attack in a person that would be undetectable during an autopsy. She claimed he also bragged about killing former patients, and attempting to kill his mother. He even allegedly admitted that his brother Roy didn't commit suicide, but that Martin murdered him because he was a drug addict, and an embarrassment to the family.

Anna's testimony was scrutinized harshly by the prosecution, as she had been diagnosed with dissociative identity disorder, and had e-mailed the lawyers in the case several times attempting to get them to investigate something she had dreamed about, or submit her dreams into evidence. She was essentially undermined as a credible witness, and her testimony was taken with a grain of salt, rather than being the damning evidence it could have been.

The stories Anna told were not completely out of left field, though. Martin was known to have little patience for his family's addictions. When his daughter Vanessa came to him seeking help for a drug problem, he advised her to take her own life to avoid embarrassing the family further. It is not outside the realm of possibility that Martin wanted his addict brother out of the way, and may have had a hand in his death.

Gypsy's roommates testified that she was getting increasingly agitated with Michele's existence, and began planning ways to get her out of the way, so she could be with Martin.

Gypsy Willis herself testified against Martin in the murder trial in exchange for a lesser sentence on charges she was facing. It was revealed that Gypsy had gone under a handful of assumed names in her life, mainly in order to evade taxes, and to hide from authorities on charges related to evading taxes.

On November 9th, 2013, Martin was found guilty of the murder of Michele MacNeill, and of obstruction of justice for attempting to cover it up.

In December 2013, while awaiting sentencing on his charges, Martin attempted suicide in prison. He dismantled the disposable razor that qualified inmates have access to for 15 minutes a day, and used it to cut his femoral artery. Sergeant Spencer Cannon of the Utah County Sheriff's Office said Martin "was unhappy he was interrupted", and was "not cooperative with treatment efforts".

Michele's sister, Linda Cluff, said, "It is a cop-out. I believe that it is not about remorse for any actions that Martin did. I believe that he is incapable of feeling remorse. He has put himself in this situation and he is realizing that there is the great possibility that he may spend his life in prison."

In July 2014, Martin faced a separate trial for sexual assault charges against his daughter, Alexis. A few weeks after Michele's death Alexis twice woke to her father fondling her. Martin claimed he thought she was her mother. Alexis decided to come forward to make sure her father was brought to justice for all his wrongdoings, and to protect others from possible future abuse.

This assault was far from Martin's first. His professional career was plagued with accusations of assault and rape. Many women came forward after Martin's arrest to tell the family of the abuse he put them through. The jury only took two and a half hours to find him guilty on sexual assault charges.

Martin's daughter Rachel said, "He really knew who he could take advantage of. I thought I had an idea of who my father was, but I had no idea. The father that I knew was a fictional character. It was an act the whole time."

In September 2014 Martin was sentenced to 15 years to life in prison for the sexual assault of Alexis, 15 years to life for murder, and of 1-15 years for obstruction.

On April 9th, 2017, Martin MacNeill committed suicide in prison using a natural gas line from the prison greenhouse where he worked tending to the plants.

THE MURDER OF THERESA FERRARA

41

NATALIE FOGEL

Theresa Ferrara and the Lucchese Crime Family

New York in the 1970's was certainly one of the most crime driven cities in the world. The Lucchese family was one of "The Five" families that dominated the organized crime scene in this era. In fact, this family still holds great power today. Becoming involved with this family was never a matter of "if" you would run into problems, but rather "when". Through countless, calculated murders, crimes, and street wars, this family soon came to be feared by everyone that wasn't "made" or an "associate." Ultimately, the story of Theresa Ferrara is officially unsolved. What is fact and proven true is that Ferrara was involved and a major pawn in much of the Lucchese crime activity in the 70's. Her demise is one of great tragedy and a picture of what lengths the Lucchese family would go to in order to protect its goals.

Theresa Ferrara was not the typical Italian-American female. She was born in Long Island, New York in 1951. She was a gorgeous young woman who could hold her own in nearly any situation. To say that Mafia traditions were in her blood is a true and most literal statement. She was a relative of New Orleans crime boss Carlos Marcello. She did, however, have modest early goals for her life.

Ferrara moved to Queens, New York in her late teen years. She had long dreamed of being an actress and a model as a teenager. She had much support from her family in this endeavor. After all, her family new the possibilities of what may happen if she went down a path that others in her family had. Theresa would soon happen in to the Mafia circle by circumstance, rather than by her own initial intuition. An introduction at a bar in Queens, New York would ultimately start her path to a horrific fate.

The Lucchese family was one of "The Five" families that ran New York at this time. This organized crime ring was and still is a nationwide phenomenon known collectively by the group title as The Mafia. Among the five families, each had a share of New York that would control nearly every aspect of its area. Businesses were made to pay "dues" to the family whose area they were located in. This was not an optional due as the result for not paying said dues would not be a pleasant punishment. Drug deals that were so typical of the street life had to go through the family. Deals that didn't go through the family would, again, have a punishment that would result in a gruesome death. Certain police members were even bribed by these families in order to protect their business endeavors in the city. The police force typically abided in some shape or form out of greed and sometimes fear.

The Lucchese crime family had an order similar to other Mafia families at the time. Membership in this family was straightforward. A "made man" was one that could have his Italian descent traced back to the "homeland", as Italy was referred to by many. These men typically had groups within the family whom they controlled. A made man could not be touched, at least by the book standards. A made man could kill, ultimately, without question or reason if he felt it would advance or enable successful business. Clearly, made men had high influence and decision making power. An "associate" was a member of the crime family who did not have the full Italian lineage. While associates were not the ultimate decision-makers, these men still had vast amounts of power and stood on a step just slightly below a made man.

To expand this order further, families of the members were also awarded certain protections and exclusive rights. This has both pros and cons in the order of the Mafia. While families could thrive off of a luxurious lifestyle, protection from rivals, as well as having overall power, the negative actions or impacts of a member would commonly affect the members' whole family. In other words, if the family felt it was necessary to "whack", or kill, a member who had messed up or they needed gone, the entire family of that member would be in danger as well. These relationships and social order within the Lucchese family is crucial to understand in order to comprehend the path of Theresa Ferrara.

By 1972, Theresa Ferrara had been established in Queens for over 4 years. She was just 21 years old when she would meet a man that would change her ambitions forever. On a fateful night in Queens at one of the many Lucchese controlled bars, Ferrara was approached by Tommy DeSimone. Theresa was a highly attractive young woman, catching the eye of most any man she walked by. Tommy DeSimone was a married man. He was also a very powerful Lucchese family associate. The two soon would start an affair that would involve her in the Lucchese family affairs. All of the powerful players within the family quickly learned about Theresa. She was lavished with a lifestyle fit for a queen. While she and Tommy were not officially together, she was accepted into the lifestyle by this circumstance. She soon was a regular at the Lucchese hangouts. The infamous Robert's Lounge in downtown as well as The Suite, run by Henry Hill. She was quickly becoming involved in a life that was very familiar to her.

Over the next five years, Theresa Ferrara started making her money in much more daring ways than modeling. She quickly became a small quantity drug dealer. She was well known as a local cocaine and Quaalude dealer in the Lucchese owned areas of Queens. Not only did she sell drugs to every day residents of the area, she was selling drugs to Tommy DeSimone and other powerful Lucchese family members as well. This was obviously a risky endeavor. She even opened up her own MOB beauty salon in Bellmore, Long Island. In addition to doing Lucchese stylings, she was also selling drugs from her shop. While abiding by Mafia rules, she soon would attract unwanted attention. While some police officers could be bought, not all of them had a price tag. She was arrested in the summer of 1977 in her shop. She was charged on numerous counts of drug possession, smuggling, and distribution among many others. She would be facing a lengthy sentence. In just five years after entering the criminal lifestyle, she was facing the possibility of spending her best years in a jail cell. That is, if she couldn't find a way out of it.

Ferrara had been caught in the act. There wasn't a lawyer on the planet who could be successful in defending her charges. She had sold drugs out of her salon to an undercover Drug Enforcement Administration agent. Facing certain extended prison time, she agreed to cooperate with authorities. The Lucchese crime family was soon to be probed from within.

It was late in 1977 that Theresa Ferrara began to really gamble with her life. She knew that, as a cooperating witness who was feeding much needed evidence against the Mafia underworld, she would be afforded certain "protections" in her daily life from the FBI. Not only did she know this, she took great advantage of it. She began to rob many other successful salons in New York. The New York Police Department was forced to turn a blind-eye to this, as the FBI had abruptly ordered them to leave it alone. To law enforcement, getting the "big fish", in this case the Lucchese family, behind bars was priority number one, two, and three.

In 1978, Ferrara had begun to fully understand just how protected she was. When she had met Tommy DeSimone in 1972, she had immediately surrounded herself with numerous mob bosses and associates. Among these associates was a man named Richard Eaton. The significance of their relationship would come to a head in 1978, when he and Ferrara began to conspire to go after Lucchese money itself. The pair allegedly conspired to steal $250,000 worth of cocaine from a shipment that would arrive in Ft. Lauderdale, Florida. This was obviously a risky move, but by this time Theresa was fully working as a willing informant. It is crucial to remember that Theresa was not a member of the Lucchese family. While she had trust from the family due to her relationship with several associates, she did not have an integral role in the big operations that the family was executing. When Theresa conspired to steal from the Lucchese family, she was not acting on FBI orders. She was taking advantage of her government induced protection.

If this decision wasn't a risky enough gamble for Theresa, she had to go bigger. It was in December of 1978 when Ferrara and Eaton conspired to steal a hefty portion of the money stolen by the Lucchese family in the world famous Lufthansa Heist. Like many other crimes, the FBI could not solidly prove that this happened. It would essentially seem an odd coincidence that Ferrara moved to the North Shore Towers in Great Neck in January of 1979. This duplex would cost her $1500 per month just for rent. This was an extraordinary price for a 27 year old, single woman who was working in a salon and executing small time drug deals. If this seemed out of the ordinary for the people around her, it must have seemed very suspicious to the Lucchese family, especially at the time when money had disappeared and several deals had been tipped off to law enforcement. Even before the Lufthansa Heist, the family was becoming deeply suspicious of several people, perhaps none more than Theresa Ferrara.

Roughly a month before the famous Lufthansa Heist, Ferrara tipped off the FBI on a massive drug deal that was to go down. In November of 1978, the FBI and DEA brought down a drug smuggle of epic proportions. 30 tons of cocaine was intercepted at the Queens Waterfront. Theresa Ferrara was solely responsible for tipping the agents off. The drug smugglers were said to be the Lucchese family leaders of Jimmy Burke, Paul Vario, and Tom Monteleone. The FBI had long wanted to take down Paul Vario, who was the financial brains it seemed of the family. Jimmy Burke was a powerful family boss who controlled a large area within the family reaches. Tom Monteleone was another boss for the family. These three men were furious when this shipment was intercepted. Paul Vario and Jimmy Burke were set to make $300,000 each off of this deal. This started suspicion among the entire family. The men knew there was a "rat" in their ranks. Even so, they were set to soon pull of one of the most notorious heist in United States history. This heist, ultimately, would cost Theresa Ferrara her life.

The Lufthansa Heist was an elaborate and well executed theft of enormous proportions. Depicted in many pop culture classics, these events go far beyond the crime itself. To understand the fall of Theresa Ferrara, the Lufthansa Heist is the single most important event to follow.

Lucchese crime family associate Jimmy Burke had planned the heist. Burke was easily one of the most powerful people in the Lucchese crime family, even though he could not be a "made man" due to his lineage. The heist planning started when Jimmy Burke's associate, the infamous Henry Hill, was given valuable information on millions of dollars in unmarked bills. These unmarked bills, as he was told, were flown in from West Germany once a month. This money was tourist money and as well as exchanges by military members of the region. The currency was flown in on a Lufthansa, the largest German airline for the time period. The money would then be stored in a vault at Kennedy Airport, where it would soon be transferred to its next destination. Jimmy Burke and Henry Hill were confident they could pull a heist off at the point just before the transfer from the vault. The informant, Louis Werner, was an airport worker who owed a Lucchese family book keeper, Martin Krugman, over $20,000 in gambling debts. Pleading for his life, Werner desperately gave this valuable, classified information to the family. The blue print for the plan had been set in motion. The execution would be one of the smoothest and skilled in United States history.

On December 11, 1979 the Lufthansa Heist began. At 3:12 A.M. cargo agent at the John F. Kennedy Airport noticed a black Ford van suspiciously backed up to the ramp door. He went over to investigate and was violently attacked. The two men, oddly not wearing any masks or gloves, pulled his hat over his eyes before hitting him multiple times in the head with pistols. He was thrown into the back of the van where another man was waiting for him.

"They threatened me. They told me they knew what I was about and that they knew where my family lived," cargo agent Kerry Whalen said. "They said they had others ready to go visit them."

With this chilling ultimatum, Whalen nodded his head to show that he understood. Senior agent Rolf Rebmann heard the noises that resulted coming from the loading ramp. He went out to investigate. He was met by six masked men brandishing powerful firearms. These men forced their way in and handcuffed Rebmann. Using a key that Werner had earlier provided, the men made their way with a bloodied Kerry Whalen and a handcuffed Rolf Rebmann through a maze of hallways and doors. They rounded up the two other employees and took them to the cafeteria. Information provided by the informant, Louis Werner, allowed the men to know what employees would be working and where they would be located. Without this information, it is likely they heist could not have worked.

There were six other employees eating their lunch in the cafeteria. The gunmen showcased the bloodied Kerry Whalen to the employees, perhaps in an effort to dissuade any of them of trying to resist. Nine of the ten employees were bound and gagged and made to lie on the cafeteria floor. One of the men, wielding a shotgun, was to keep look over these employees.

John Murray, another senior cargo agent, was forced to call Rudi Eirich on the intercom. Murray was forced, at gunpoint, to lead Eirich to believe there was a problem with the incoming load from Frankfurt. He was instructed to meet Murray in the cafeteria. This is significant to the Lucchese family because Rudi Eirich was the only security guard on duty that morning who knew the code to the double-door vault holding the money.

Eirich arrived to the cafeteria only to see all of the other employees bound and gagged on the floor as well as six men wielding shotguns. One man was to stay behind to keep eyes on the employees, while the other men took Eirich at gunpoint to the double-door vault.

Eirich would later testify as to how knowledgeable the men were to the vault. The double-door vault had a system to where both doors could not be unlocked at the same time. The robbers knew this and were very meticulous as to how they would continue the heist once inside the first door.

Rudi Eirich was forced to open the inner door first. This door led the robbers to a 10 ft. by 20 ft. room filled with all the goods they were seeking. There were hundreds of parcels available for the taking. Being as they were loading this into a single van, they had to make sure they took the right parcels. They searched through the invoices and freight records and decided on the packages they would take. They knew in all of this that if Eirich opened the second door, the alarm would sound. They bound Rudi to the floor as they executed the first part of their plan.

The men began to toss 40 parcels through the first door. This was done in less than 4 minutes. After this was complete, Eirich was untied and made to lock the inner door before unlocking the outer door. Once the inner door was locked and the outer door was opened, two of the men began to load the van with the 40 parcel haul. Eirich was again tied up and locked in the vault. With the van loaded, the men returned to the cafeteria at 4:14 A.M. They ordered the employees to call Port Authority Police at 4:30 A.M. and not a second before. Having their lives and the lives of their families threatened, the employees obliged. The robbers left the employees at 4:16 A.M. The men left the airport, with all cash in tow in the van, at 4:21 A.M.

The Port Authority Police were not called until 4:30 A.M. This was crucial to the heist. Had they been called immediately when the robbers left, the building would have been under lock down within 90 seconds of the phone call. This information was valuable to the Lucchese family. This information was, again, obtained by the informant Louis Werner.

The robbers, having made an efficient and safe getaway, arrived at a garage in Canarsie, Brooklyn. Waiting for the van at the garage was none other than Jimmy Burke and his son Frank. The money was transferred from the van to another vehicle. This vehicle would be driven by Jimmy and Frank to one of the Lucchese family holdings. The other men were instructed to drive home. The driver of the get a way van, Parnell "Stacks" Edwards, was supposed to take the van used in the heist to a New Jersey auto yard and have the vehicle compacted and destroyed. When Jimmy and Frank arrived at the safe house to count the money, Jimmy was shocked by the haul. Expecting just over 2 million dollars, he was surprised to learn that the robbery had yielded them over 6 million dollars. This was the largest heist, at that point, on American soil ever recorded. To put the heist into another perspective, this was all achieved in just 64 minutes with no murders and no gun fire. Extensive planning and use of insider information led to one of the greatest crimes in history.

How does Theresa Ferrara fit into all of this? If she was an FBI informant at the time of the heist, why did she not tip off law enforcement? The events after the heist are nothing short of amazing. The murders that occurred at the hands of the original boss and leader of the heist were the direct result of paranoia. A key mistake made by Parnell "Stacks" Edwards would lead to the eventual murders of 10 integral members and perhaps dozens more that were not directly tied to the heist.

Jimmy Burke, Lucchese associate and crime ring leader, became increasingly suspicious of those around him. He was hell bent on eliminating anything or anyone that could lead police back to him for the heist. The year following the heist became known as the Witness Elimination Program. While not everyone was killed, anyone who made even the slightest misstep or raised any suspicion at all with Jimmy Burke was murdered. Police would be on a while goose chase from December 1978 to June 1979. The newspaper was regularly riddled with bodies, bloodshed, and mystery. The entire essence of organized crime in New York was facing the possibility of being completely dismembered as a result of the heist.

The key mistake made in the heist was, ironically, not a part of the heist itself. Parnell "Stacks" Edwards had a fairly simple job. He was the get a way driver of the van in a chase that never happened. He smoothly had to drive the fan to the garage. His main task was to get rid of the van after the transfer was made at the garage. Even for this, Jimmy told him exactly where to go and how simple the process would be. Not only did Edwards not take the van to the New Jersey auto yard for scraping, he didn't get rid of the van at all. He was obviously excited about the successful heist, and decided to celebrate by smoking marijuana on his way to the wrecking yard. In his confusion, he drove to his girlfriend's apartment and managed to leave the fan in a no parking zone. He spent the morning snorting cocaine and getting drunk with his girlfriend, fully intending to take the van to the auto yard later that day. Little to his knowledge, police had impounded the improperly parked van and quickly discovered it was the van used in the robbery. Edwards left the complex without being apprehended, however his fingerprints were found on the steering wheel. A muddy shoe print, found at the airport on the concrete surface, was matched with a shoe inside the van. This shoe also belonged to Edwards. For all intents and purposes, Parnell "Stacks" Edwards was officially a dead man walking.

The FBI, immediately following the heist, had narrowed it down between two major crime groups to blame for the Lufthansa Heist. The first group was the John Gotti crew, and the second was the Jimmy Burke crew. Burke had long had a reputation as a mastermind who was a stone cold murderer. The knowledge that was required to complete this heist led investigators to initially favor that it was, in fact, the work of Jimmy Burke and the Lucchese crime family. When Parnell "Stacks" Edwards made his mistake, police had the evidence they needed to go after the Jimmy Burke crew further. Edwards had long been a patron at Robert's Lounge, a well-known Burke gang hangout.

The FBI aggressively started a detailed procedure to investigate the Burke gang and try to gather enough evidence to obtain a warrant. They were constantly watching all of the known hangouts of Jimmy Burke and his crew. They bugged vehicles, tapped phone lines in establishments, and they even bugged the pay phones around the hang outs. They famously followed the gang in helicopters on numerous occasions. This was all common for Jimmy Burke and his gang in the months following the heist. Activity by police started as soon as the van was impounded in the days following the heist. This would trigger a deadly race between Jimmy Burke and the FBI. Jimmy knew that the police were on him, largely due to Edwards' mistake. Jimmy Burke would start a killing spree at this time in an effort to kill any witnesses and accomplices that he deemed suspicious. Parnell "Stacks" Edwards would be first.

Parnell "Stacks" Edwards was murdered execution style in his apartment just seven days after the heist. The shooters were two of Jimmy Burke's most trusted men: Tommy DeSimone and Angelo Sepe. These two men were largely believed to be involved in hundreds of murders over the years as ordered by Jimmy Burke and other Lucchese family associates. Angelo Sepe was believed to be the primary killer in the Witness Elimination murders as also ordered by Burke.

Tommy DeSimone, former boyfriend of Theresa Ferrara and valued member of the Jimmy Burke crew, was about to face the punishment for breaking the Mafia order. Earlier in 1978, DeSimone had murdered two valued "made men" of the Gambino crime family. Murdering made men was an especially deadly idea. No later than January 14, 1979, DeSimone was tricked into arriving at a Gambino location to be "made." Little did he realize, he was being lured in only to be assassinated. He was shot in the head and the face upon walking through the front door. Even worse for Jimmy Burke and the Lucchese family, they could not seek retribution for this as Tommy DeSimone had murdered "made men".

On February 10, 1979, Theresa Ferrara received a phone call at her salon from a caller that was unknown to all but Ferrara herself. "I have a chance to make $10,000," Ferrara told her 19-year-old niece Maria Sanacore. Theresa informed her that she was going to a nearby diner in Long Island. It struck Sanacore odd when Theresa told her that if she wasn't back in 15 minutes that she needed to come looking for her. Theresa Ferrara left the salon in a hurry, leaving behind her purse, car keys, and extravagant mink coat. This would be the last time she would be seen alive by anyone but her murderers.

On May 18, 1979, a female torso was found floating in Barnegat Inlet. This inlet is near Toms River, New Jersey and in the heart of much organized crime. The torso was not only dismembered completely, it was utterly unrecognizable. An extensive autopsy was performed. The body was identified through a recent breast augmentation. This was the body of Theresa Ferrara. No one has ever been convicted of the crime. There was simply no evidence. To understand who committed this, and why this was committed, it is important to understand the other murders in the Witness Elimination killings.

On January 6, 1979 Martin Krugman, the first to tip off Henry Hill and Jimmy Burke of the opportunity to plan the Lufthansa Heist, was murdered and dismembered in Vincent Asaro's fence factory. Hill later claimed that the remains of Krugman along with several others were buried under Robert's Lounge. Krugman was a book keeper for Jimmy Burke's gang and famously owned a wig shop and men's hair salon. He was ultimately murdered for his intense demands for his share of the heist money. Fearing that he would eventually tell investigators information on the heist, Burke had him killed.

On January 17, 1979 Richard Eaton was tortured and murdered by Jimmy Burke himself. Richard Eaton had teamed up with Theresa

Ferrara earlier in 1978. Eaton was a con artist and an associate of Burke. He had no direct involvement in the Lufthansa Heist. He was caught with "fake cocaine" and running a scam while skimming money from the Lucchese family. Essentially, laundering money from the powerful family while selling a fake product. He also was skimming vast amounts of the Lufthansa Heist money using the same process. Theresa had proven involvement in this scam. She and Eaton had planned it out and knew what the Burke gang had done. The suspicion of the FBI is that Eaton, in an effort to save his own life, blamed the scam on Theresa Ferrara. In any event, the involvement of Ferrara and Eaton was known by the Lucchese family and Jimmy Burkes crew. His body was famously hanged in a meat freezer for investigators to find. This especially caught the attention of media and dominated headlines for many days in New York.

The next murder on the Witness Elimination timeline was that of Theresa Ferrara. She was next in line after her scam partner Richard Eaton. While still unsolved with no convictions, it is just one of several murders that happened in this killing spree with no solution. The Richard Eaton murder, however, would prove to have devastating consequences for Jimmy Burke.

In March 1979, the third accomplice of Theresa Ferrara and Richard Eaton was murdered in Florida. Tom Monteleone was accused of being involved in the scam as well, laundering the money through the Player's Club, a local bar that hosted Burke and his crew. This bar was owned by Monteleone.

The murders of Monteleone and Richard Eaton were essential evidence to FBI personnel that Jimmy Burke was responsible for the murder of Theresa Ferrara. However, they had no evidence and, with the subsequent murder of all the witnesses, would struggle to find the necessary evidence.

Over the next few months, five more witnesses would be murdered at the hands of Jimmy Burke and his crew. The effort he took to eliminate witnesses that could lead to his conviction in the heist was nearly successful. While most all of the murders were officially unsolved, there was one murder that could leave Jimmy Burke on a one-way trip to prison. That murder was none other than Richard Eaton's.

In 1982, Jimmy Burke was sentenced to 12 years in prison for his involvement in the Boston College point shaving scandal. While in prison, it is widely understood that many cohorts of Jimmy became more comfortable to talk. Through very secretive and reliable investigation, Jimmy Burke was charged with the murder of Richard Eaton while serving his 12 year prison term. He was sentenced to 20 years to life. Jimmy would eventually contract lung cancer and die in prison in 1996. He was 64 years old.

Henry Hill, the right hand man of Jimmy Burke, was largely the contributor to the ultimate murder conviction of Burke. Facing charges and a possibility of facing serious jail time, Hill cooperated with police. Henry Hill knew if he went to jail, his family was in serious danger. For his information, Henry Hill was admitted to the Witness Protection Program with his family. He died in 2012.

The fates of nearly all of those involved in the heist were dreadful. While murders were confirmed by police, more than half of the slain bodies were never found. The bodies that were found typically were put in place because the Mafia families wanted them found. Most of the money obtained in the heist was predictably put back in to the streets or in casinos or drugs. While police didn't solve most of these murders, the perpetrators usually received their own fates by other members. To pull off one of the most lucrative heist in history, there is understandably going to be collateral damage. However, this amount of damage was near total.

Theresa Ferrara was just 27 years old when she was murdered. Pursuing a modeling and acting career, she moved to Queens. Her story, while one of tragedy and sadness, is largely a result of her own decisions. Ultimately, she tried to scam one of the most powerful families in New York, and her fate was sealed. The nature of chasing a dream and living a lifestyle is a complicated one. Who you surround yourself with will largely determine your lifestyle. For Theresa Ferrara, she surrounded herself with MOB associates and criminal bosses, and eventually she was dealt a hand that she wouldn't survive.

BUMPY JOHNSON

Ellsworth Raymond Johnson was called"Bumpy" by most. The nickname is the first of many mysteries surrounding the Harlem legend. Some claim he got the name as a child due to a bump on the back of his head. Others say it comes from his violent reputation and refers to him "bumping off people." Others still claim Johnson gave himself the name, referencing his ability to "bump people around" on the basketball court. Some have another nickname for Bumpy, to this day, they refer to him as the "Godfather of Harlem."

Bumpy Johnson was many things in his life, to many people. He was a stick up man, a burglar, a pimp, a drug dealer, a numbers runner, a bookmaker, a hood and a thug. He was also a husband and a father and a doting grandfather. He was the conduit between Harlem and the Genovese Crime Family. He was a respected friend of Lucky Luciano. He was a man of Harlem, giving to the needy, the hungry, and children. He was a staunch advocate for education, urging neighborhood children to stay in school and make something of themselves. He was a friend to the actors, starlets, and musicians who came from Harlem and who spent their late nights partying there. He spent time with the activists of the era, such as Malcolm X. He was a legend, all of Harlem knew him, many of Harlem still do. Yet, he never rose to the stature of fame that so many other gangsters of his era did. He was all these things, but he was also a private man, one who kept his secrets close, and to this day it is hard to find much information on him.

Johnson was born in Charleston, South Carolina on October 31, 1905 and spent most of his childhood there. He was not born to a poor family, instead his family was relatively middle class for the time period in the South. A smart boy, he had skipped two grades by the time he was 8 years of age. When Bumpy was only 10 years old his older brother, Willie, was accused of the murder of a white man. Bumpy's parents, fearing southern justice in the form of a lynch mob, sent Willie up north to live with family. Four years later Bumpy was showing all the signs of having a temper worse than his brother. Fearing Bumpy's insolence towards whites they sent their son off to live with his elder sister, Mabel, in Harlem.

While living with his sister Bumpy graduated from Brooklyn's Boy's High. He then went on to attend City college for a few semesters. While in college Bumpy set his aspirations high and studied pre-law. Finishing college wasn't in the cards though. Bumpy fell in with a rough and wild crowd. He left school and began a career in robbery and burglary. He found that he had quite the talent as a stick up man. His penchant for violence and other criminal activities caught the eye of Madame Stephanie St. Clair.

Stephanie St. Claire was one tough lady. Outside of Harlem she was known as "Queenie" but the people of Harlem referred to her as Madame St. Clair. St. Clair had been associated with the gang "The Forty Thieves" until she decided to branch off on her own. With 10,000 dollars of her own money St. Clair started her own numbers game, and took over Harlem with authority. The Madame dominated the numbers racket and much of the other criminal enterprises in Harlem. In fact, she ran one of the biggest and most profitable numbers operations in all of New York City. Bumpy began working for St. Clair as a leg breaker and enforcer. Of course, he was quite good at making sure the message was received when he paid someone a visit. He quickly became a trusted associate of her's, rising fast in the ranks. Eventually he became her principal lieutenant. Though she was 20 years older than Johnson, many believed the two were lovers for sometime.

Bumpy was no stranger to the wrong side of the law or prison. When he was released from Sing Sing in 1933 for an attempted grand larceny conviction he had already spent nearly half of his life behind bars. He wasn't even 30 years old yet. His proclivity for violence towards both inmates and guards caused Bumpy to be transferred frequently to different prisons. Thoroughout his criminal career he would spend time in Sing Sing, Alcatraz, Leavenworth, and Dannemora Prison. When he left Sing Sing he was broke and desperate for employment. He went back to working with St. Clair. And, it was upon that release that would begin to his ascent from criminal to legend and folk hero.

While Johnson was in prison Jewish mobster Dutch Schultz had moved in on the entire Harlem territory. Most of the Harlem bookmakers had turned their racket over willingly to Schultz, as they had no interest in a war. Madame St. Clair and a few others were still holding out. With Bumpy now out of prison and back at the Madame's side they waged a violent war against Schultz.

The war for control of Harlem was a bloody one. Over 40 people were murdered. Several kidnappings occurred. It was also a very lopsided war. Bumpy and St. Clair were ruthless and smart. However, Dutch Schultz had both connections in City Hall and had the backing of several Mafia allies. With control over police protection also in Dutch's back pocket Madame St. Claire, Bumpy and the other independent operators in Harem stood no chance. Dutch managed to gain and keep control over Harlem and its profitable numbers racket.

That should have been the end of it, and likely no one would remember Bumpy Johnson. Fortunately for Bumpy and St. Claire Dutch Schultz was a wild card with a terrible temper and poor impulse control. Dutch was federally indicted numerous times and becoming the prime target of the federal government and United States Attorney Thomas Dewey. Sensing weakness in Dutch's operations, and assuming a conviction was imminent, the Luciano and Genovese family began to move in on his territory, claiming they were only going to "watch over it" in case Schultz was sentenced to prison.

The relationship between Lucy Luciano and Dutch Schultz was one of mistrust. Luciano knew Schultz's reputation for violence and had no doubt that Dutch would try to take his territory back by force when an opportune moment presented itself. Not shockingly Luciano had little interest in giving Dutch back his very profitable territory. The opportunity never came. Schultz sought permission from the Mafia Commission to assassinate U.S. Attorney Dewey. The commission refused to approve the move. They felt an assassination of a federal attorney would bring too much unwanted federal attention to the entire organization. When Schultz left the meeting in a violent rage Luciano saw his opportunity to cement his family's control over Dutch's former operations.

Luciano ordered a hit on Dutch Schultz and he was gunned down on October 23rd, 1935. The moment was sweet revenge for St. Clair and Bumpy. While Schultz lay dying in the hospital St. Clair sent him a telegram. It read simply, "As ye sow, so shall ye reap."

Bumpy's moment to ascend to legend would very soon come. In 1940 Johnson met with Lucky Luciano and made a deal with the Italian Mafia that would stand for the next 28 years. The deal gave St. Claire, Bumpy, and the other Harlem operators who had fought with them control over the Harlem numbers racket once again. Bumpy reused to negotiate on behalf of those Harlem operators who had handed their operations over willingly to Dutch, he had no interest in helping those who refused to fight for themselves. Bumpy's and the others operations would still participate in the Mafia's central gaming pool and Johnson became the conduit between Harlem and the Italian Mafia. In addition all of their operations were now under the protection of Luciano himself.

This bold move made Bumpy an instant folk hero in Harlem. No other black man had been able to step up and cut a deal with the Italians. That he had the courage to even attempt to meet with the Italians was stunning. That he met with the Italians and came away with a deal and their respect was the stuff of legends. It wasn't long after St. Claire and Bumpy regained control of the Harlem numbers racket that St. Claire decided to retire. She gave her entire operation to Bumpy. Bumpy Johnson was now the uncrowned crime boss of Harlem. From this point until his death no one could or would dare to run an illegal operation in Harlem without clearing it with Johnson first, and cutting him in, of course.

But, Bumpy Johnson didn't just negotiate a deal with Lucky Luciano. He built a relationship with the mob boss. The two often played chess together. At one point Johnson was sent to Dannemora, where Luciano was already serving time. The two were often seen talking, and in one instance Bumpy saved Luciano's life, preventing him from being shanked. Two years before Luciano died in 1962 e sent a wooden hand carved chess set to Johnson's wife. Many would later claim that Luciano and Johnson were not friends, but when you talk to those that were close to either there is much evidence they had a mutual like and respect for each other

Just because Bumpy had a good relationship with the Italians didn't mean he laid down for them. His primary concern wasn't pleasing the mafia, but instead looking out for the people of Harlem. In one instance some Italians began to move in on one of Bumpy's bankers. In response Bumpy called a meeting of all the bankers, controllers, and runners of Harlem. What was said specifically in the meeting is unknown, but it lasted 3 hours. The next day the result of the meeting became clear. More than half the runners for the Italians called in sick. Those that did come to work seemed to be working at a slower than leisurely pace. The receipts for that day dropped drastically and the point was made to the Italians. Luciano set a meeting up with Bumpy in Luciano's suite in the Waldorf Astoria. The two men met and talked and the issue was settled and Bumpy's people went back to work.

In another incident members of the Italian crew came into Harris's Bar in Harlem and dragged out one of the customers. No one in the bar dared make a move to stop them, as interfering in mob business rarely ended well. Someone did run to tell Bumpy, and when he couldn't be found he was phoned at his house. After getting all the information he could, Bumpy jumped in to his car and drove off. An hour later the kidnapped man was free and strolling back into the bar he had been dragged from earlier. Somehow, even though the man had made some kind of mistake with the mob, Bumpy was able to use his pull to get him off. That was Bumpy, he was able to his power and the respect he had earned from the mob. This was just one more thing that made him someone not to be underestimated or to be messed with.

Known for being a dapper dresser, Bumpy was often seen out and about in a black suit, complete with a tie and a black Fedora. Though he was a smaller man, standing about 5'8" and weighing around only 170 pounds Bumpy Johnson was feared for a reason. He was almost always armed. He carried both a knife and a gun on him at almost all times. His temper and penchant for violence was well known and well documented. During one of his many prison stays Johnson spent 3 years in solitary confinement for his violent behavior against other inmates and even the guards.

Another well shared story regales the day Bumpy beat a man in a night club. The man was badly injured and taken to the hospital. That should have been the ed of it. Hours later, however, Bumpy was told the man intended to rat him out to the authorities. Enraged, Bumpy rushed to the hospital and beat the man again, while he was on the operating table, while shocked Doctors and nurses watched.

Though he was never arrested for killing anyone, no one doubts that Bumpy was capable of murder, or that he may have been behind more than a few. He didn't shy away from violence, nor did it effect him. While waiting for his table at a restaurant Bumpy attacked a rival, almost gouging out one of his eyes and badly beating him. After beating the man witnesses claim Bumpy calmly stood up, straightened his tie, and inquired if his table was ready. Bumpy is said to have told those with him he suddenly was in the mood for spaghetti and meatballs. When necessary the man could have ice in his veins.

Bumpy often told people he was a barber. He is even listed on the 1940 United States Census as one. His granddaughter, Margaret, has joked that he was in fact quite skilled with a straight razor. Of course he wasn't giving haircuts. In the early 1930s Bumpy went after Ulysses Rollins, an enemy enforcer, with a switchblade. He slashed the man over 30 times. Rollins was lucky to survive.

Bumpy wasn't just unafraid of getting violent to handle things, he also had little fear of death or being harmed. In one incident a man cut Bumpy off while he was driving his Cadillac, then stopped his vehicle, jumped out of his car and began firing at Johnson. Unarmed at the moment, an unphased and unafraid Bumpy jumped out of his vehicle and began running at the man shooting at him. As the bullets flew past him Bumpy kept running towards the man. Likely shocked, and a little scared, the man stopped firing and ran back to his car, getting in and driving off before a very angry Johnson could reach him. After this incident some would say Bumpy scared people so much they couldn't even shoot straight when facing him.

To many, including Bumpy himself possibly, the man must have seemed immortal. Many expected him to meet a violent end. It wasn't for lack of attempts. Over his lifetime he had been shot, stabbed, and assaulted. But, Bumpy always survived. While other mobsters, gangsters, and mafia men met untimely ends Bumpy Johnson wouldn't die and he wouldn't stay down.

In 1948 Bumpy had just finished yet another prison stint. This time he had served 10 years at Dannemora in upstate New York. Bumpy walked into a diner on Seventh Avenue and saw Mayme Hatcher sitting alone and eating. While she ignored him, he was intrigued and sat down at her table. The two talked for a while, and Mayme was so taken with Bumpy they left the restaurant together and went to the movies. The two were together from that point on. A month later Bumpy proposed. The two were on a drive when he looked at Mayme and told her "You and I ought to get married". She simply responded, "is that so?" Two months later they were married in a small civil ceremony. Meeting in April and marrying in October, the two would be together for the rest of Bumpy's life and Mayme would speak lovingly of Bumpy until she died in her early 90s.

Their life was one of luxury. Bumpy's criminal enterprises provided them with more than enough money. They lived in spacious, beautiful apartments. They traveled to Europe. Bumpy bought Mayme several furs, she could have anything her heart desired. Many women were jealous, many women tried to steal him away. But, Mayme would always be Bumpy's girls.

The couple raised their two daughters together, both girls were from previous relationships. Ruthie was Mayme's daughter but Bumpy loved her as his own. Mayme in turn loved Elease, Bumpy's daughter as her own. The two also raised their granddaughter, Margaret, as their own. Bumpy doted on all three girls. The girls had lavish birthday parties complete with pony rides. There was nothing he wouldl deny them. They often went to Aqueduct and Belmont to place bets on the horses. Bumpy even had chauffeur driven limousines take the girls to private school.

It was 3 years after Bumpy and Mayme married that Bumpy had his closest brush with death. Bumpy was at an after hours club on West 122nd, The Vets Club. It was close to 5:30 a.m. when a drunken Robert (Hawk) Hawkins strolled up to the bar. Hawk was a wannabe pimp, a young loud gambler from North Carolina. He was looking to make a name for himself, though many believe he didn't immediately realize it was Bumpy standing at the bar. Bumpy was near Hawk and overheard him speaking vulgarly in the presence of a friend's girl and a few other women. Bumpy scolded Hawk when he cursed in front of the women at the bar. In spite of his bad ass reputation, Bumpy abhorred cursing or smoking in front of women.

The two exchanged words and Hawk left drunk, embarrassed, and angry. He returned an hour later, having borrowed a revolver from a friend. A very quick struggle ensued. Bumpy managed to hit Hawk with a potted plant as Hawk fired off one shot at him. The bullet meant for his head hit Bumpy in the chest and bumpy fell to the ground. For a moment Hawk likely though he had killed the legend. But, Bumpy opened his eyes and Hawk ran from the bar. Bumpy stood slowly. The owner of the bar and a bartender drove Bumpy to Sydenham Hospital on Manhattan Avenue.

The bullet struck less than an inch away from Bumpy's heart, and surgery took 6 hours. By the time Mayme Johnson made it to the hospital many of Bumpy's friends and associates were also there. The police were there too, desperately trying to get Bumpy to tell them who had shot them before he possibly slipped away for good. Mayme shooed the police away and prayed for her husband. The doctors were uncertain Bumpy would survive. Bumpy was in a coma for 5 days. During that time the nuns of the neighborhood church lit candles for his recovery, indeed all of Harlem waited with baited breath to see if the Godfather would pull through. There was an endless procession of visitors to the hospital. Many nurses would later tell of how often and well they were slipped cash by the gangsters and mafia that came to visit, they all wanted to see Bumpy well taken care of. When he did at last open his eyes he gave his wife a weak smile, and then began humming "It Had to be You." Yes, Bumpy had survived.

Bumpy Johnson wasn't just a violent gangster. He was a complex character, one that was loved just as much as he was feared. He may have been a "tough guy" but he was also well known by Harlemites for his generosity. Some referred to him as the "Robin Hood of Harlem." He loved to help the poor in the community and was known for his gifts and the cash he freely gave to them. During the depression he sponsored neighborhood bread lines. He gave turkeys to the poor in Harlem at Thanksgiving. He also sponsored many neighborhood block parties. He would pay the rent of those about to be evicted. If ever there was a need Bumpy was there to help. He may have taken from the community but he never hesitated to give back to it.

It was children that held a special spot in Bumpy's heart and he showed it in his generosity. Every Christmas Bumpy spent thousands of dollars on presents for the children of the neighborhood. He would help with school clothes, books,money for shoes, whatever the children of Harlem needed. Often, he would be spotting strolling down Lennox Avenue deliberately and noisily jingling the change in his pocket. Behind him a small horde of children would follow. Bumpy would walk into the ice cream shop and order a dish of vanilla ice cream for himself, and then grandly gesture to the kids behind him, "Give them whatever they want" he would state.

Bump's generosity wasn't just in nature. It was also a good business decision made by a very smart man. The good will his many good acts bought him made it easier for others to turn a blind eye to his criminal activities. Bumpy was a giving man who loved children and took care of the poor. He refused to curse or smoke in the presence of women he didn't know. He was also a mobster, a pimp, a robber, and the king of all of Harlem's illegal enterprises. It was his intelligence and fearlessness that made those two personas work so well together.

During his total 26 years in prison Bumpy furthered his education. He loved reading, and was known to read and quote literature often. Bumpy also found an interest in poetry. He even wrote some poetry of his own, pieces of which were later published during the Harlem Renaissance. Bumpy was a skilled chess player. He loved literature and it is said his library at his home was more than extensive. The Harlem mobster could even read Latin.

Later in life Bumpy did attempt to go legit, or at least he steered a portion of his empire legitimate. He became the proprietor of an insect extermination company based in Manhattan. However, in 1952 Bumpy was brought up on federal charges of conspiracy to sell heroin. Though he was convicted, Bumpy maintained his innocence, claiming he was framed. Johnson was sentenced to 15 years and sent to Alcatraz. Even in Alcatraz Bumpy found a way to further his legendary status. A well-believed rumor has Bumpy helping 3 inmates escape, arranging for a boat to pick them up. This escape was the first, and only successful escape from Alcatraz, and of course Bumpy had a hand in it. Johnson, himself, stayed put and was released from Alcatraz in 1963.

Arrested more than 40 times Bumpy was no stranger to the law. He wasn't afraid of the law either. In 1965 Bumpy Johnson staged a sit-down strike at a police station to protest what he felt was excessive surveillance of himself and his associates. Refusing to leave the police station he ended up being arrested. He was brought before a judge on charges of refusal to leave a police station. The judge acquitted him.

Bumpy wasn't just respected and even loved by the people of Harlem. He also rubbed elbows with many celebrities. Johnson was known to hang out with Bill "Bojangles" Robinson and Billie Holiday. Not only was he friendly with the great Lena Horne, many believed he had a brief fling with her. He was also a good friend of Sugar Ray Robinson. He was the godfather of Sydney Poitier's eldest daughter. Bumpy interacted with just about anyone who was anyone from Harlem.

He was also a good friend, supporter, and protector of many black activists. He and Paul Robeson were good friends. It was Bumpy and his associates who went and rescued Paul from the violent riots in Peekskill. Bumpy also offered both protection and other services to Malcolm X just days before his assassination. Bumpy felt strongly that Malcolm should respond with violence to the threats against him. Malcolm declined, stating he didn't want to see "black folks killing black people." Days later Malcolm was dead, assassinated. Bumpy was said to have been quite upset that Malcolm didn't take him up on his offer of protection, feeling he could have saved him.

On July 7, 1968 after eating dinner with Mayme the two sat down to watch The Laurence Welk show. Bumpy got up and said he was heading to bed. A few moments later he changed his mind deciding to go out instead. He said good night to his wife and left with his childhood friend Junie Bryd. He took $500 cash with him. He and Junie went to a card game. After Bumpy had lost almost all of the money he brought with him he left the game alone. It was around 2 a.m. when Bumpy Johnson walked in to Wells Restaurant in Harlem. He ordered his usual, a fried chicken leg, hominy grits, and coffee. The waitress had just brought his food and he had just begun to eat when Bumpy fell to the floor, shaking and clutching his chest. A nurse, who happened to be there eating rushed to try to help. Finley Hoskins, a long time friend of Johnson, was there, and rushed to Bumpy's side as well. Someone ran from the restaurant to get Junie Bryd, who was at the Rhythm club down the street. Bumpy was alive, but not conscious, when Junie got there. Cradling Bumpy in his arms, Bryd watched as his good friend opened his eyes for a moment and smiled. And then Harlem's Godfather died. It wasn't bullets or a knife or at the hand of a rival that Bumpy Johnson left this world. Instead, he died of a heart attack in the presence of two of his closest childhood friends.

Bumpy Johnson's death and funeral was headline news. The headline of *Amsterdam News read,* "Bumpys Death Marks End of Era." The church was full. So full, that the crowd spilled out onto the street for several blocks. It seemed that everyone in Harlem was in attendance. Bumpy had touched that many lives.

Before her death in 2009 Mayme Johnson was vocal about her husband's legacy. She wrote her own book, prompted in large part, by the portrayal of her husband in the movie "American Gangster." Frank Lucas claims that Bumpy was a mentor to him and that he became Johnson's second in command. Lucas also claimed that Bumpy died in his arms, yet it is well known he didn't. In fact, Mayme asserts that not only did Bumpy not trust or like Frank Lucas, but that he was no where near the restaurant where Bumpy died on the night of his death. Mayme further asserts Lucas wasn't even at Bumpy's funeral. She also said that while Frank Lucas may have driven Bumpy on occasion there was no way he was her husband's driver. Bumpy preferred to drive himself. In addition he wasn't out of prison for 15 years so Lucas's claim he was his driver for 15 years is impossible. Mayme asserts that Frank Lucas is a liar, and that Bumpy knew that, referring to him as such when he was alive. Frank Lucas may have been in Bumpy's life but he was not part of his inner circle. Instead, according to his wife, he was a wannabe and a hanger on, who assumed everyone who knew better was likely dead.

"American Gangster" wasn't the first time Bumpy was portrayed in a mainstream movie or media. He may not be nearly as well known as many gangsters of his time but he still popped up often in movies and television. He is the inspiration for the character, Bumpy Jonas in "Shaft." In "The Cotton Club" the great Laurence Fishburne plays a character based off Johnson, Bumpy Rhodes. The movie "Hoodlum" portrays the struggle for control of Harlem between St. Claire, Bumpy, and Dutch Schultz. Once again Bumpy is played by Fishburne. Mayme Johnson has said that Hoodlum didn't get everything right. However, unlike "American Gangster" she felt that the inaccuracies were accidental, and they didn't bother her. She notoriously proclaimed she would never see "American Gangster" because if Lucas had lied about his relationship with her husband he had likely lied about everything else in the movie as well.

Bumpy Johnson was a private man. Even though his legend lives on there is little on paper about him. His own granddaughter turned to a genealogy website in hopes of finding more information about the man who raised her and loved her. Most of his close associates are dead and gone. His wife and daughter are both now dead too. He was respected, revered, and feared. When he was alive he owned Harlem. Many of the long time residents of Harlem knew of him, and there are many personal stories and legends about the man. Yet, once he was gone his reputation never rose to the status of many of the mobsters almost everyone knows by name. But, Bumpy was a private man, and likely he would have wanted it that way.

BLACK WIDOW JUDY BUENOANO

ERIN CARTER

Judy Buenoano loved men. But she loved killing them more.

In 1971, she murdered her husband James and nine years later she would kill her own son, Michael. In 1983, she would attempt but fail to kill her boyfriend, John Gentry. She is also believed to have been responsible for the death of Bobby Joe Morris (another boyfriend) in 1978. She was never convicted of the Morris crime, however, as by the time the authorities had connected the dots she was sentenced to death for the murder of her first husband.

But the suspicions didn't stop with the Morris death. Buenoano is also suspected of killing a man in 1974 and in 1980, another boyfriend would die under suspicious circumstances.

Buenoano would become the first woman executed in Florida since 1848 and only the third woman executed since capital punishment had been reinstated in 1976.

She would be sent to the electric chair in 1998. Her last words were that she wanted to be remembered as a "good mother."

Instead, she would go down as one of the most sadistic female serial killers in American history.

This is her story.

EARLY LIFE

Judy was born Judias Welty in Quanah, Texas on April 4th, 1943. Her father was a day laborer at a local farm. Judy would talk about her mother being a full-blooded member of the Mesquite Apache tribe but little did she know that a "Mesquite Apache" tribe didn't exist.

Her mother would die of tuberculosis when Judy was only two years old. She and her baby brother Robert would be sent to live with their grandparents while their two older siblings would be put up for adoption.

"When Judy's mother died," forensic psychologist Paula Orange said. "It sent Judy's life into a tailspin. This is one of those 'Butterfly Effect' scenarios. A tragic circumstance that occurred early in a child's life that led to her perpetuating pain on everyone else for the rest of her own adult life."

She would eventually leave her grandparents and join her father in Roswell, New Mexico. He had remarried and Judy would claim that both he and her new stepmother would beat, starve, and burn her with cigarettes.

They made her a "house slave", forcing her to do chores around the house at their bidding. Judy would finally act out at the age of fourteen as she would burn two of her step brothers with hot grease. Not stopping there, she attacked both her father and step-mom with fists flying.

Police would be called and Judy would be jailed for over two months. After she served her jail time, the judge gave Judy a choice, either return home or go to reform school. She opted for the latter and was sent to Foothills High School. She would remain there until 1959 when she would graduate at the age of sixteen.

She held her entire family in contempt, particularly her younger brother Robert.

"I wouldn't spit down his throat if his guts were on fire," Judy once said when asked about her brother.

CHANGING IDENTITY

Judy returned to Roswell but changed her name to "Anna Schultz". She found work as a nurse aide and would give birth to a baby boy out of wedlock, Michael Schultz on March 30, 1961. Judy would remain silent on the identity of the baby's father but people believed that Judy was having an affair with a pilot from the nearby air force base.

In 1963, the twenty-two-year-old Judy would marry James Goodyear. Goodyear was twenty-nine years old and serving as a sergeant in the United States Air Force.

They would have their first child together, James Jr, four years later. James would celebrate the event by legally adopting Michael. Daughter Kimberly would come a year later as the family would move to Orlando, Florida.

Judy would then open her own business, starting the Conway Acres Child Care Center in Orlando. She listed James as the co-owner even though he was during a one-year tour in the Vietnam War. After returning home, he only had three months of downtime before he was admitted to the U.S. Naval Hospital in Orlando, complaining from symptoms staff physicians never quite identified. He would die on September 15, 1971.

Goodyear was only thirty-seven years old at the time of death and authorities believed he died due to natural causes.

"He came home from Vietnam ill and he never got well," Judy said. "It had nothing to do with me. I was not in Vietnam."

"Crazy that Goodyear was able to survive the horrors of Vietnam but not Judy Buenoano," Orange said. "He had no idea he was married to a sociopath. She had no respect for the fact that he had just put himself on the line for her and the country. All she saw were dollar signs."

Judy poisoned James with arsenic and waited almost a week after his death before cashing in his three life insurance policies. A few months later, an "accidental fire" burned down their Orlando home. Judy would receive another $90,000 in fire insurance.

She lost her husband and her home. But her purse was never fatter.

NO GRIEVING WIDOWS ALLOWED

Judy would waste no time finding another man. Despite having three kids in tow, she would find a new love in Bobby Joe Morris when she moved her family to Pensacola.

It was business as usual for Judy as she had a fat bank account courtesy of James Goodyear and a new beau in Bobby Joe. Eldest son Michael, however, was not doing well in school. He scored on the low end on IQ tests and was a behavioral problem. Judy would get him evaluated at a state hospital in 1974 and then sent Michael out to foster care where he would also receive psychiatric treatment.

Judy's new home would suffer another "accidental fire" and she collected money from the insurance. She then took Michael out of foster care and moved to Trinidad, Colorado with Bobby Joe and the rest of her children. Judy then changed her name from "Anna Schultz" to "Judias Morris".

FOUR YEARS MAX

Judy would date Bobby Joe for four years before deciding it was time to cut him loose.

Bobby Joe would start to suffer from the same mysterious illness as James Goodyear did years earlier as he complained of dizziness and vomiting. He would be admitted to San Rafael Hospital on January 4, 1978, but doctors would not be able to pinpoint what was wrong with him. He would be sent home to Judy's care two weeks later. Two days later, however, he would would pitch face-first into his dinner plate, unconscious. He would be rushed to the hospital, but Judy knew that her "medicine" had taken effect.

Five days later, Bobby Joe Morris would be dead. Doctors would chalk up his death to cardiac arrest and metabolic acidosis.

Judy would wait, just like she did after she killed James, before cashing in on Bobby Joe's life insurance.

Authorities were none the wiser.

But Bobby Joe's family suspected something fishy was going on. Back in 1974, Judy and Bobby Joe had been visiting Brewton, Alabama when a man from Florida was found dead in a motel room in that town. Police would find the man in the room after receiving an anonymous call. He was shot in the chest with a .22-caliber weapon and his throat was cut open.

Judy's connection to the crime? Bobby Joe's mother had overheard Judy telling her son about the murder.

"The sonofabitch shouldn't have come up here in the first place," Judy said. "If he came up here he was gonna die."

Bobby Joe had told his mother about the crime on his deathbed. She thought the confession could be attributed to his delirium, but Bobby Joe told her too many specifics to ignore.

"We should never had done that terrible thing," Bobby Joe mumbled to his mother. "Never should have done that to him."

She tipped off police but they would not be able to find any fingerprints inside the room and no bullet was recovered from the corpse. The case remained unsolved.

WHAT'S ONE MORE SURNAME?

On May 3rd, 1978, Judy would change her name again. This go around, she would change her last name to Buenoano, which in Spanish meant "good year." She stated that she meant it as a tribute to her husband James Goodyear and her Apache mother.

Things continued to go bad with Michael as he dropped out of high school in the tenth grade. With limited employment opportunities, he would join the army in June of 1979 and get assigned to Ft. Benning in Georgia after basic training. When he was on his way to his new post, he visited Judy in Pensacola.

Judy greeted her son with open arms. Then she began poisoning him.

By the time he reached Ft. Benning, he felt sick. Army physicians would find seven times the normal level of arsenic in his body.

They could do little to reverse the damage done. Six weeks after his arrival, the muscles in his arms and legs and deteriorated to the point where he was a paraplegic.

"Michael had no use of his legs," Orange said. "And he could not move his arms past his elbow. Again, Judy was a sociopath. It is unfathomable for a normal human being, a mother, to do this to her own child. Yet she did it to Michael. He was always an inconvenience to her but now that he had military insurance he could become an asset in death."

Judy would give Michael the short shrift while favoring James and Kimberly. Michael and James didn't get along well as clearly their mother favored the latter. Judy would hide Michael when people came over because she was ashamed of him. She would have a neighbor named Constance Lang watch over him when visitors arrived.

"Michael didn't fit the picture Judy wanted to present to the world," Orange said. "She wanted to be looked at like a woman of high status. She drove a Corvette and owned her own business. Michael was a slow-thinking kid. She didn't want anyone to see that."

The army didn't investigate the reasons behind Michael's inordinate levels of arsenic. Instead, they set him up with leg braces and a prosthetic device on one of his arms.

He would be discharged from active duty because of the medical disability.

But his mother saw dollar signs.

The day after his return home, Judy wasted no time. She organized a fishing trip with Michael, James, and daughter Kimberly. They would leave Kimberly ashore at the East River bridge while they went into the water with a two-seat canoe. A small folding lawn chair had been placed in the middle of the canoe for Michael who had was outfitted with a leg brace, a fishing reel, and a ski belt.

James would state that had fished for about two hours when they were reaching shore when a "snake fell into the canoe." He said that everyone panicked as the snake slithered around. The canoe hit a log and capsized.

James would claim to have been knocked out by the impact and would remember nothing until he came to inside an ambulance.

He would tell this version to the court but when he was talking to Army investigators, he made no mention of a snake.

"There is conjecture as to how much James was involved or much did he know," Orange said. "The statement given to the army investigators is different from what he would state later in court. The statement given to the army was a written statement and the handwriting didn't seem to match his own."

A man named Ricky Hicks saw the overturned canoe, an ice chest, and a plastic bag in the river. He also saw Judy and James.

"I lost the other boy," Judy said as Ricky approached them on the shore. "A snake had gotten into the canoe and I tried to hold the snake down with a paddle."

"Where is he?"

"It's no use," Judy said, waving him off.

Hicks said Judy appeared to be concerned about James then asked him for a beer. He then drove Judy's car to a nearby phone and called the county rescue squad.

The rescue team arrived and began looking for the missing Michael.

The canoe had not moved as there was barely a current. They would find Michael's body one-quarter of a mile upriver where the canoe had been rescued. The rescuers stated that it should not have been a problem to swim upstream, suggesting that Michael could have been saved.

Judy initially said that Michael had a life jacket on but later recanted and said that it was a ski belt.

There was no ski belt on Michael when he was found.

Judy would later state that after the canoe capsized, she saw James lying face down in the water. She swam over and cleared his air passage to resuscitate him. She looked around for Michael then was picked up by Ricky Hicks.

"Michael disappeared under water," Judy said. "I went to rescue James. I almost lost both of my sons that day. Mothers just don't murder their children. If I'd have lost both of them, I don't know what I would have done. They would have had to put me in a mental institution."

"Kimberly's boyfriend would later testify that Judy had killed Michael for the insurance money," Orange said. "The children knew about their mother but she had clearly brainwashed them into silence. She provided for them, she fed them. She knew what was best."

Telling the police that she was a "clinical physician", they bought her story of the boat capsizing. The army investigators did not buy her account. Not having any evidence, however, they would eventually pay her Michael's military life insurance ($20,000). Investigators got suspicious, however, when they found out that two civilian life policies were taken out on Michael. The applications on both policies look to have been forged.

Judy's former sister-in-law, Peggy Goeller, would call to inquire how she was doing. She would make no mention of Michael's death during her first call but on a second call she told Peggy that Michael had died "during Army maneuvers".

MOVING ON

Judy would demonstrate very little grief over Michael's death and she would not be charged with his murder. Foremost on her mind was finding another man and another big check.

She opened a beauty salon in Gulf Breeze and found her next mark: businessman John Gentry.

Gentry was more well-heeled than her previous conquests so Judy put on airs for his sake. She told him that she had Ph.D.'s in biochemistry and psychology and was the former head of nursing at West Florida Hospital.

Gentry believed her story and decided to spoil his blue-blooded girlfriend expensive gifts, vacations and the finest cuisine all in the name of courtship.

Pushing the envelope, Judy would encourage John to provide life insurance for both them both. She then secretly boosted Gentry's coverage from $50,000 to $500,000 without him knowing.

Two months later, Judy began giving Gentry "vitamin pills".

"Come on," she said, placing two pills into Gentry's palm.

"What are you, my mother?" Gentry asked.

"Well, God forbid I want to see you healthy," Judy slid the cup of water toward her prey.

Gentry would then complain of dizziness and later begin vomiting after his daily dose of Judy's "vitamins."

He would admit himself into the hospital and noticed that his symptoms disappeared when he stopped taking the vitamins.

Still smitten by Judy, he did not suspect her of wrongdoing. Instead, he took her vitamins and hid them in his briefcase.

One night, however, Judy sat him down for a special dinner. She had a very special announcement.

"I'm pregnant," she said, smiling in triumph.

"Finally," Gentry said. He told Judy that they should celebrate. She told him to go to the liquor store for an expensive bottle of champagne.

"Be right back," he said, kissing her with excitement.

Running out the door, Gentry got into his car and a bomb exploded with he turned the ignition key.

Amazingly, Gentry survived the blast as trauma surgeons saved his life.

"Judy really overplayed her hand with the explosion in the car," Orange said. "Really it speaks to her level of dedication and ingenuity. Who knows where she got the idea, maybe watching the Godfather. But the police found the dynamite residue inside Gentry's car. They decided to look no further than to Judy herself."

Their interrogation and research would unearth lie after lie. They found out about the $450,000 increase in Gentry's life insurance.

Gentry himself thought the insurance had been canceled. He was shocked to learn that she had increased the payout and was paying his premiums out of her own pocket. The police didn't spare him any quarter. They would him that she was not a real doctor and that she couldn't get pregnant.

"What?" Gentry muttered, completely flabbergasted.

Judy had been sterilized seven years earlier.

Gentry couldn't believe his ears. Police would go on to say that she had booked tickets for a world cruise for herself and her children...leaving Gentry out. They discovered that Judy had been telling her friends that Gentry was suffering from a "terminal illness."

The only "terminal illness" Gentry had was Judy Buenoano.

Now fully convinced, Gentry would reach into his briefcase and give police the "vitamin pills" that Judy had been giving him.

"Judy was emptying the vitamin casing and filling it with formaldehyde and a little arsenic," Orange said. "Over time, this would have been lethal."

The state attorney would refuse to charge Judy as they wanted an air tight case in order to prosecute. Knowing that they had their killer, officers, and federal agents searched Judy's home in Gulf Breeze, obtaining wire and tape from her bedroom that looked to match the same wire/tape they found on the bomb in Gentry's car.

They would search her son James' room, finding marijuana and a sawed-off shotgun. He would be jailed him for possession of drugs and an illegal weapon.

"Again, this is a strange mistake on Judy's part," Orange said. "She was meticulous and a good liar. Why she didn't remove any and all evidence from her home is a head-scratcher. She had gotten sloppy because she had gotten away with so many crimes before without so much as a slap on the wrist. She thought she was above the law, got careless and left incriminating evidence behind."

Judy would then be arrested at her beauty salon and charged with attempted murder. It took a month of police work, but authorities would trace the source of the dynamite used in the bomb, linking the Alabama buyer to Judy via phone records which showed numerous long-distance calls from her home.

Judy would pay bail but authorities would not let up. Five months later, she would be indicted for first-degree murder in the death of her son Michael, with an additional count of grand theft for the insurance scam.

Feeling the noose around her neck, Judy would fake a seizure and wind up in Santa Rosa Hospital.

Authorities then exhumed the bodies of the men they believed she killed. Bobby Joe Morris was exhumed with arsenic found in his remains. Identical results were obtained with the exhumation of James Goodyear, in the following month.

Connecting the dots, police obtained a court order to exhume the bodies of all the men that had died while associated with Judy; son Michael, husband James Goodyear, and boyfriend Bobby Joe Morris.

Arsenic would be found in all of the bodies.

"There was enough arsenic in him (Goodyear) to kill twelve people," Detective Ted Chamberlain said. "So he was loaded. I mean that boy was loaded with it when he went down."

OPEN AND SHUT CASE

In 1984, Judy would be convicted of the murders of Michael and attempted murder of Gentry. In a separate trial in 1985, she would be convicted of the murder of James Goodyear in which she would ultimately receive the death sentence.

Judy would be imprisoned in the Florida Department of Corrections Broward Correctional Institution death row for women.

HER FINAL HOURS

Judy would spend her last day watching a hunting and fishing show, eating chocolates, and talking about old times with her children and cousin Jeanne Eaton. She would read a suspense novel called "Remember Me" and her last meal with be steamed broccoli, asparagus, strawberries and hot tea.

Judy's impending execution did not receive the same media attention as Karla Faye Tucker whose was executed only a month earlier. Her execution was opposed by the Pope and Jesse Jackson.

'"She may not have been as photogenic, as young or as pretty as Karla, but she was just as good a Christian," Eaton said.

"Judy obviously had her enablers within her family," Orange said. "How could she be 'just as good a Christian' if she is poisoning people, blowing them up and the 'Christian' she is being compared to is ice-picking people to death. People say the strangest things."

But Judy herself was bitter that no one paid much attention to her presence on death row, particularly the fact that she was a woman.

``Karla was a young female, very attractive and she had become a Christian in prison," Judy said. ``We all prayed that she would be granted a stay of execution and clemency because we felt that she was a different person and she deserved a chance. Possibly, I am a different person. But I was a Christian when I came here. I was a devout Catholic. I've not changed in that."

"It was a bit of a curiosity as to why the media was so charged to prevent the execution of Karla Faye Tucker and paid little heed to Buenoano," Orange said. "Tucker's killings were ferocious and sadistic while Buenoano's killings could be seen as passive. But what drew people to Tucker was her physical appearance and demeanor. She came across as a sweet, reformed choir girl at the end. She had a charming smile and a soft voice. Buenoano, on the other hand, looked sinister. She had squinty eyes, high cheekbones and a snarling, Southern drawl. Her body language and demeanor screamed hostile."

Judy would enter the death chamber with several guards by her side. They strapped her into the large oak chair, placing leather straps over her waist, wrists, chest, and legs.

They fitted the calf and headpiece electrodes last, inserting a wet sponge in between to reduce the burning of Judy's skin.

"Do you have a final statement?" the warden asked.

"No, sir," Judy closed her eyes tight.

The witnesses on the other side of the glass partition watched in silence.

Judy did not look at them as a leather mask was placed over her face.

The warden nodded his head and the switch was pulled.

Steam wafted up from her right leg as her body jolted for thirty-eight seconds. Her hands balled into fists, white knuckling from the shock as smoke rose from her feet to the ceiling.

Then Judy went limp. She would be pronounced dead at 7:08 a.m., March 30th, 1998.

The date was her son Michael's 37th birthday.

BLACK WIDOW KRISTIN ROSSUM

AIMEE BAXTER

Photos of a beautiful, lively little girl, her blonde hair in pigtails as she dances The Nutcracker in her little pink tutu. That same adorable child laughingly enjoying holidays with her family at their home. These are the pictures that Constance Rossum will show you of her daughter Kristin.

Bright, vivacious, and uncommonly beautiful are the words used to describe Kristin Rossum as a child. The child that everyone said was so smart and pretty, the one who modeled for department stores and who excelled in her schoolwork, the one with what seemed to be the perfect suburban childhood.

However, as many already know ... looks can be deceiving.

Idyllic Child becomes a Rebellious Teen

Born to Ralph and Constance Rossum on October 25, 1976, in Claremont, California, Kristin Rossum wanted for nothing. Kristin was the first child of Ralph Rossum – a professor at Claremont McKenna College – and his wife Constance – who worked at Azusa Pacific University. Even when her first and then second little brother was born, Kristin remained her parent's sweet little princess.

When Ralph accepted a position as President of Hampden-Sydney College in southern Virginia, the family moved across the country from California to Virginia. It was 1991 and Kristin was a delicate 15 years old. Her parents enrolled her in an all-girl boarding school in Richmond, Virginia named St. Catherine's School.

That seems to be the beginning of the end of Kristin's innocence. At the private school, Kristin made friends quickly and soon was very popular. She became the party girl smoking, drinking, and using marijuana liberally.

In 1992, at just 16 years old, Kristin is introduced to methamphetamines – a strong Central Nervous System (CNS) stimulant – and is soon hooked. Within a few weeks, she was using Crystal Meth (also known as Crank, Speed, Chalk, etc.) daily. She was a tweaker (slang used to describe a methamphetamine addict).

Kristin the Druggie

When asked about it later, Kristin recalled her first time using meth by saying "I remember it feeling good, a kind of euphoria. You feel very revved up and energetic and happy. I wanted to feel that all the time."

Soon, Kristin's straight As were slipping to become Cs and Ds. She lost weight rapidly and began to withdraw from her family and any friends who were not using meth. According to later court records, Kristin is described as having "an almost insatiable need for crystal meth."

It was not long before Kristin developed all the character traits that addicts hone to conceal and continue their freedom to use. Lying, manipulation, and theft became the new norm for young Kristin Rossum.

Her parents were understandably at a loss for how to deal with this behavior. After all, not that long ago they were tucking her into her pink canopy bed and kissing her goodnight with a song and a prayer. However, the lack of consequences established by her parents could be a contributing factor in her later misdeeds.

At first, they ignored their daughter's erratic and rapidly devolving character, chalking it up to teenage angst. Eventually, they could not turn a blind eye anymore and they soon realized that their daughter was not who they thought she was.

Later, both Ralph and Constance cite an incident in 1993 as the first time they admitted their daughter had a problem. After returning from a cruise in April of that year, the Rossums found that their sweet, perfect daughter had in fact stolen their credit cards, personal checks, and a video camera.

Confronted with the missing items, Kristin pointed to some of her friends (fellow druggies) as the thieves. They say that she admitted to using some of the cash to buy drugs but insisted that the rest was stolen by somebody else. Her parents accepted Kristin's excuse and did not report the theft to police.

According to Constance's testimony later, Kristin's erratic behavior came to a head in December of 1993. Ralph Rossum – convinced Kristin was still using drugs – attempted to search his daughter's backpack. She resisted, they struggled, and he struck her several times in the arm to get the bag away from her.

However, that was not the end of the incident. Sobbing and enraged, Kristin grabbed a knife from the kitchen and slashed at her wrists. When that did not work, she ran upstairs to the bathroom, locked herself inside, and began hacking at her wrists with a razor. Later Kristin told the court, "I felt devastated

... I didn't know how to deal with the situation ... I wanted them to see how sorry I was."

Her wounds, however, were superficial and her parents treated them at home. They later said that they were "afraid of what would happen if they took her to the hospital." They feared that if they told the hospital that she had cut herself, they would have committed her for a psychiatric evaluation and if they tested her blood and found drugs, they would report her to the police.

It is likely that the reason none of the cuts were serious was that Kristin did not intend them to be. Psychologists later speculated that it was merely a way for her to manipulate her parents. If it was, it worked.

Again, Kristin escaped any immediate consequences for her bad behavior. Again, her parents made excuses for her behavior and thus enable her to continue that behavior. Cryptically, one entry in her diary after this incident contained the morbidly, prophetic words, "I could get away with murder."

A few days after this incident, a teacher noticed the marks on Kristin (or she possibly showed them to her intentionally). She called the police to the school to investigate the possibility of child abuse.

Officer Larry Horowitz of the Claremont Police investigated and testified that Kristin told him that her father had hit her and that her mother had "called her a slut and said she was worthless." After interviewing Ralph and Constance Rossum, Officer Horowitz concluded that there had been no abuse and the case was closed.

In January 1994, Constance found a glass pipe hidden in Kristin's underwear drawer. She eventually called Officer Horowitz and Kristin was handcuffed, arrested, and held for several hours at Claremont Municipal Jail.

Kristin finally had her first taste of culpability. She seemed to clean her act up and after graduating, she enrolled part-time at the University of Redlands in California. However, soon she relapsed and dropped out of school without a word to her family and simply disappeared. She moved to Chula Vista – a suburb of San Diego near the Mexican border.

A Chance Encounter

After a month of hard partying, drinking, smoking meth, and hiding from her parents, Kristin was walking the pedestrian bridge that led from Chula Vista to Tijuana, Mexico. Authorities speculate that at the time she was likely on her way to meet her supplier in Mexico on that fateful day.

As she crossed the bridge, Kristin Rossum dropped her jacket. Before she could retrieve it, a handsome young man that she later described as reminding her of John Stamos, had picked it up and was handing it to her. It was Greg de Villers and he later told friends "it was love at first sight." They chatted in French while Greg's younger brother paced nearby.

She returned to the Southern California apartment where de Villers lived with his brothers, Bertrand and Jerome, and a friend, Christopher Wren. She never left.

Within a few weeks, the couple was professing their love and de Villers had sworn to help Kristin kick her meth addiction. Greg's brothers and Wren were not happy and prompted him to end the relationship. They had noticed that things were coming up missing from the apartment since Kristin's arrival and knew of her drug problem.

According to a statement given later by de Villers' friend and roommate Christopher Wren, Kristin had told him that she felt like being with Greg was the wrong choice. For some reason, Wren chose not to tell his buddy.

Even if Wren had told de Villers about Kristin's doubts, it is unlikely that it would have made any difference. Greg de Villers was adamant, he loved Kristin Rossum no matter what her faults and he was going to save her from herself.

By May of 1995, it looked as though he had done just that. By all accounts, it looked like Kristin was clean and free of the hold meth had on her. She reestablished contact with her worried parents and it looked like Kristin was finally moving towards the bright future her parents had envisioned for their little girl.

The Rossums looked at Greg de Villers as if he was an angel for all that he had done for Kristin. Constance Rossum, in an interview with the CBS news magazine "48 Hours," put it like this, "We always called Greg our godsend from heaven. I mean, of all the people she could have met, to have met a nice, decent person who wanted to take care of her, we thanked God."

Soon, Kristin enrolled at San Diego State University. Her professors later said described Rossum as a stellar student with one going so far as to describe her as "among the most promising students" he had "ever taught."

Everyone who knew her believed she was happy. She was earning straight As and in 1998, she graduated cum laude (with honors). She got a job at San Diego Medical Examiner's office as a toxicologist.

Constance would later testify, "Our old Kristin was back," and she thanked God and de Villers – in that order – for the change.

Storybook Love?

Everyone who knew them described Kristin and Greg as the perfect couple. Constance Rossum testified later that when they were together they were "like a couple of lovebirds." When they announced their engagement, nobody was surprised.

However, as is often the case, outward appearances did not accurately represent reality. There was a layer of tension beneath the surface of de Villers and Rossum's storybook love affair. Kristin's closest friends knew that she had a hard time staying faithful and monogamous.

According to prosecutor's later, Kristin actually maintained a "graphically flirtatious" correspondence with a former boyfriend and at least one other man during at least some portion of her relationship with de Villers. Rossum even went to her mother only a month before she was supposed to walk down the aisle and broke down in tears as she told her mother that she wanted to cancel the wedding.

Constance Rossum considered her daughter's outburst to be cold feet, pre-wedding jitters that would pass. After all, Greg de Villers was the man who led her out of the darkness of addiction and Constance could not see how Kristin could possibly want to end the relationship.

She would soon tell the court, "I gave her the wrong counsel, I'm afraid."

The wedding was spectacular. The video shows a smiling and laughing Kristin Rossum, now Kristin de Villers, dancing with her new husband and looking happy. As for de Villers, he is recorded on that video saying, "Kristin is the most wonderful person I've ever met. I just can't wait to spend the rest of my life with her."

Only seven months after the wedding, however, Kristin Rossum told her mother that she felt "trapped like a bird in a cage." It was January 2000 and Kristin's journal shows that she had begun souring on her marriage only a couple of months after the wedding.

Greg de Villers did not show any sign that he felt the same or even knew of his wife's misgivings and doubt. Conversely, his brother Jerome later testified that Greg was ecstatically happy and never spoke of anything even smacking of marital discord. Even his colleagues at a genetics research firm where de Villers worked, described him as happily married and devoted to his wife. Some even went so far as to describe Greg de Villers as "sickeningly in love with his wife."

Friends of Greg de Villers said that he was often talking about his plans for their future together. He bragged about his wife's accomplishments, both big and small, and often spoke of starting a family. One friend remembers him saying that he wanted "all girls who were as beautiful and smart as Kristin."

At the same time, his adored wife was painting a much grimmer portrait of her marriage and her husband. She often complained to colleagues and friends about Greg, saying that he was moody, controlling, and domineering. Later, in an interview with "48 Hours," Kristin said, "Greg became very, very clinging... I tried to pull away and have some sort of independence."

An email sent to her brother Brent only 11 months after the wedding showed how she truly felt. She wrote, "I should have trusted my own instincts and called off the wedding. Now I'm stuck with the heavy realization that I married the wrong person."

A New Love Affair

Not long after Kristin Rossum sent that email to her brother, she met Dr. Michael Robertson. Newly hired as Chief Toxicologist at the San Diego Medical Examiner's office, Robertson was Kristin's immediate supervisor and she began spending large amounts of time with him.

Soon, they were spending time together outside of work. Kristin found danger and excitement in her passionate affair with her handsome, Australian doctor – who was also married. Her husband – and the problems she seemed to have with him – disappeared from Kristin's consideration and soon she was talking with friends outside of her colleagues about the wonderful new man in her life who she described as "a big hunk of an Australian guy."

By early May, Rossum was receiving inappropriate emails and notes from her boss. A search of her desk later turned up love notes and IOUs for things such as "a night of lovemaking" from Robertson. Coworkers later reported that Robertson was often seen sauntering into work with a bouquet of flowers that would soon end up on Rossum's desk.

In June, according to court records, Kristin Rossum had given her lover a gift. A book titled "52 Invitations To Great Sex" she had inscribed on the inside cover, "Well, sweetheart, together we'll enjoy a lifetime of passion."

When asked later, Rossum said, "I felt like I was in love. It was very romantic, very exciting, very passionate."

In August of 2000, Kristin turned to her best friend, Melissa Prager. Prager later told the court that he friend confided in her that she was madly in love with Robertson but was "terrified" by the idea of telling Greg she wanted a divorce.

In October 2000, Greg de Villers was still telling his friends, family, co-workers, and anyone else who would listen about his love for his wife and his plans for their future. His brother Jerome later told the court that around Halloween, Greg was talking about his excitement over taking his future children with Kristin out to trick or treat.

However, Kristin Rossum had reached a conclusion about her marriage. She told her close friends that she was looking for an apartment and planned to leave her husband.

'Til Death Do Us Part

It is unclear how de Villers learned of his wife's infidelity and plan to leave him. Rossum has always claimed that she told Greg de Villers about the affair and that her admission launched a spiraling depression in her husband.

According to Kristin Rossum, she told her husband about Robertson and he demanded the man's phone number. When Kristin supplied the number (although why she would is uncertain), de Villers called her boss and lover and demanded that he break off their relationship.

There is no court record of a response to this demand by Robertson. However, the relationship continued.

Authorities, however, have a very different set of circumstances in mind for how Greg discovered Kristin's infidelity.

They maintain that de Villers found out about the affair on accident in the fall of 2000. This was after Kristin and Robertson were sent to Milwaukee together to attend a toxicology conference. According to court records, despite being booked into separate hotels – likely due to rumors in the office about their relationship – the duo rented their own room together and spent several nights from September 30 to October 7 together in that room.

A coworker saw Kristin at the conference during the week and noted that she was no longer wearing her wedding ring.

One of the conferences that Rossum and Robertson attended in Milwaukee was on the deadly effects of fentanyl. Fentanyl is a clear, odorless narcotic that is 100 times stronger than morphine. It is generally administered to cancer patients whose pain is not eased by other means. It is so potent that it only takes a few drops to kill.

The seminar also discussed the fact that the drug is so rarely prescribed and used that most medical examiner's offices do not test for it. Both Rossum and Robertson were well aware of the fact that their office did not test for fentanyl.

During the three years that Rossum had worked in the San Diego Medical Examiner's office, only seven cases of death by overdose had involved fentanyl. She had seen 15 patches and 1 vial of the drug in a powder form. It was Rossum's job to log and track the drugs in her logbook. It was Robertson's job to hold the key to the cabinet those substances was then stored in.

These were facts that seemed innocuous at the time but would soon hold a more serious meaning.

Returning to Old Ways

Only a day or two after returning from Milwaukee, Rossum sent de Villers an email telling him that she was taking three different prescription drugs "to help with the severe anxiety I've been experiencing as a result of our relationship. You've hurt me beyond repair."

Not only was Kristin taking prescription medications, she had fallen back into her addiction to meth. After some of the drugs went missing from her office, Robertson admitted later that he found traces of the drug in her desk and rather than turning his girlfriend in, he flushed the drugs down the toilet. Then he covered for her with his superiors.

Once again, Kristin Rossum has done something bad. Once again, somebody shields her from the ramifications of her actions. Once again, there are no consequences for Kristin's bad actions.

Severing Ties

By early November 2000, Rossum was ready to end her relationship with de Villers. She insisted she wanted only a "trial separation."

She later told detectives that de Villers literally collapsed when she told him she was leaving him. She claimed that he lay in bed for days afterward and would not communicate with her. She later told the court, "It was painful for me, too, to see someone you love hurt so much." She still never owned up to the fact that it was her own actions that caused her husband that pain.

On November 6, 2000, just after 9:15 pm, Kristin Rossum called 991.

She claimed that her husband was unresponsive and that she was doing CPR to try and revive him. When paramedics arrived, however, they found Rossum on the phone in the living room. Her husband was lying lifeless on their bed.

Gregory de Villers lay dead in his La Jolla bedroom with rose petals covering his chest. Besides his lifeless head lay a copy of his wedding picture ... less than two years old. Nearby on the floor lay a crumpled love letter from the dashing Australian doctor that was his wife's boss and lover. Beside that was his wife's discarded diary, open to an entry that she had left confiding that she felt her marriage was the biggest mistake of her life.

For all intents and purposes, it looked like a suicide. His distraught widow claimed that Greg had learned that her affair with Robertson was still happening.

However, de Villers' brother Jerome adamantly refused to accept that his brother had committed suicide. The entire de Villers family demanded an investigation. Still, the San Diego police were hesitant to open an investigation.

The Truth and Nothing but the Truth

Their opinion quickly changed and authorities soon came to suspect Kristin Rossum, de Villers' 26-year-old blonde beauty of a wife. They believed that she had used her knowledge as a toxicologist and the information that she had gleaned from working in the medical examiner's office to poison her husband.

Due to concerns over a conflict of interest, de Villers' autopsy was outsourced to another lab in Los Angeles. That lab is one of the few in the country that tests for fentanyl. They found 7 times the lethal dose of fentanyl in de Villers' system.

Two weeks after de Villers' death, the San Diego police brought Kristin Rossum in for interrogation. She reiterated to police that her husband had been extremely depressed.

According to Kristin Rossum's story, on the Thursday before de Villers' death, they struggled over a letter that she had sticking out of her back pocket. In her account, de Villers' attempted to grab the letter from her pocket and knocked her to the ground to wrest it from her. She claimed that it was the first time she had been afraid of her husband.

When he had the letter, as Rossum's story goes, he held it out and threatened to take it to his wife's office and expose the affair as well as her reoccurring meth addiction. She took the letter and shredded it but de Villers pieced it back together.

In court, Rossum's parents described the night, two days before de Villers' death, when they went over to visit the couple for dinner. Ralph Rossum testified that de Villers seemed to be deeply depressed, "a man spiraling down."

Kristin Rossum's father continued to describe how de Villers had drunk heavily that night. He drank wine and gin until his father in law had to tell him to lower his voice. Constance Rossum described Greg de Villers' voice as "fraught with melodrama" as he spoke at length about the dozen red roses that he had given to Kristin for her birthday a few days earlier.

She testified that he seemed depressed, agitated, and particularly obsessed with the fact that all but one had died and shed its petals. In a TV interview, she gave months after the death, Rossum stated, "He was making a big deal of the last rose standing. I think he was just making a statement that he knew our relationship was over."

Things rapidly spiraled from that point on. Police learned that Rossum had relapsed and was using meth again.

On June 25, 2001 – 7 months after Greg de Villers' death – his wife was arrested on charges of First Degree Murder. She spent over six months in jail and then on January 4, 2002, her parents posted $1.25 million for bail.

During the trial, the prosecution contended that she killed her husband to keep him from telling her bosses that she was having an affair with Robertson and that she was stealing meth from the office. They presented evidence that she had the knowledge about fentanyl to use it, access to the drug (remember the missing fentanyl from her office), and the motive to kill her husband.

On November 12, 2002, Kristin Rossum was found guilty of first-degree murder.

Exactly one month later on December 12, she was sentenced to life in prison without the chance of parole. She was transferred from the San Diego jail to the Central California Women's Facility in

Chowchilla California – the largest women's correctional facility in the United States.

Distant Repercussions

In 2006, the de Villers family filed a lawsuit against Rossum and San Diego County for wrongful death. They were asking for $50 million but on March 25, 2006, a San Diego jury ordered Rossum to pay more than $100 million in punitive damages to the de Villers family. The same judge ordered San Diego County to pay $1.5 million.

According to the de Villers' lawyer John Gomez, the punitive damages awarded in this case are the most assessed against an individual defendant in California history. The jury apparently awarded double what the de Villers' family was asking for due to the estimation that Rossum could make $60 million from selling the rights to her story.

The judge later lowered the awarded amounts to $10 million in punitive damages and $4.5 million in a compensatory award.

In September of 2010, a 3-judge panel of the 9th US Circuit Court of Appeals ruled that Rossum's lawyers should have challenged the prosecutions assertion that she poisoned her husband with fentanyl by demanding their own tests. Due to this, the panel ordered a San Diego federal court to hold a hearing into whether the defense's error could have affected the trial's outcome.

On September 13, 2011, the US Court of Appeals withdrew its opinion and replaced it with a one-paragraph statement that denied Rossum's petition.

Conclusion

Kristin Rossum will spend the rest of her life behind bars. She has exhausted her state appeals and the federal courts denied her petition to be heard.

Her contention remains that her husband killed himself. She further believes that he did it the way that he did to point the finger of guilt at her. She vehemently insists that she did not kill her husband.

At one point, Kristin Rossum even suggested that her lover the handsome Australian doctor might have killed her husband. He knew about de Villers' threat to expose them before his death and had access to the fentanyl.

For his part, Robertson returned to Brisbane, Australia only one month after de Villers' death under the excuse that he had to care for his ailing mother. In September of 2013, the San Diego Reader reported that prosecutors filed a criminal complaint against Robertson in 2006 charging him with one count of conspiracy to obstruct justice.

If he returned to the US, Robertson could face up to three years in prison. In 2001, Robertson was named as an "unindicted co-conspirator" in Rossum's trial.

As of 2014, Robertson was running a forensic consulting business in Brisbane.

Kristin Rossum, the sweet spoiled only daughter of college professors, who was never held accountable for her actions as she grew up will spend the rest of her days within the walls of the largest women's correctional facility in the US. She is finally going to have to answer for what she has done.

BLACK WIDOW LYDA TRUEBLOOD

JESSI DILLARD

A true "black widow"

Death followed Lyda Trueblood everywhere she went. At first glance, it may have seemed that the young woman was facing a run of bad luck – but as the run continued, suspicions began to arise.

Northeast of Kansas City, in the small town of Keytesville, Missouri, a true "black widow" was born on October 16, 1892. Over the course of her life, Lyda Anna Mae Trueblood took on seven married names, and is most well-known as Lyda Southard. However, Idaho remembers her as Lady Bluebeard – the state's first female serial killer.

"She swept the men of her choice off their feet – courted them so persistently that they could not escape," said V. H. Ormsby, a deputy sheriff from Twin Falls, Idaho. Ormsby was one of the officers who arrested Trueblood in Honolulu for the death of her fourth husband.

By the age of 27, Trueblood had already killed six people, including her own daughter. However, she would only be convicted of one murder – the poisoning of her fourth husband, Edward Meyer, in 1921.

"The marital experiences of the one-time Missouri country town girl eclipses even those of fiction. Ten years ago, while still in her teens, she was attending Sunday school and enjoying the popularity that goes with being a village belle."

Described as "pudgy faced and plain of figure," Trueblood still caught the eye of Robert Dooley, whose family was close with Trueblood's. Some said Trueblood was the most popular girl at her high school, claiming she had an "indefinable something, a spark giving off a light that draws men, by physiological and chemical attraction."

"They wasn't so wealthy, just so-so," said Mrs. Larrabee Hanson, who lived near the Trueblood family. "But they were all church-going people, devout and clean-living. (Trueblood) went to church every Sunday without fail."

A magazine writer, Alan Jaffe, who detailed Trueblood's history for a profile in *Argosy* magazine in 1957, said men "hung around her like flies about a honey pot." In fact, when Trueblood finally left her childhood home and moved to Twin Falls, Robert Dooley followed – and the two were married there in 1912, when she was only 21.

A promise of the future

"They had a perfectly normal relationship," said Mychel Matthews with the Twin Falls County Historical Museum. "They appeared to be just like the rest of the residents around town."

With the security of their future family in mind, the newlyweds decided to take out an insurance policy on Robert and his brother, Edward. If either died, the survivor would inherit $1,000 – with an equal amount going to Trueblood. And by August 1915, the couple was $2,000 richer. Edward Dooley had fallen ill and had died after just a few days – typhoid, the doctors said.

"There was nothing suspicious about the death," Matthews said. "It was ruled as food poisoning or typhoid."

As Edward lay dying, Trueblood convinced her husband to revise his insurance policy – for the family's protection, she argued. A new policy was drafted for Robert and his wife, stating that if either died, the surviving spouse would receive $2,000.

Just one month later, Robert Dooley followed in his brother's footsteps – succumbing to typhoid in a similar fashion. Trueblood, however, had begun to build herself a substantial nest egg. Only six weeks after losing her husband, Trueblood's infant daughter, Laura Marie, "drank from a contaminated well," according to reports – leaving the widow lonely and desperate for companionship.

Since accidental poisonings did occasionally occur in rural areas, and epidemics – particularly typhoid – were rampant during that time, the deaths of the Dooleys were only briefly investigated by authorities.

"Little children died all the time, at that period of history," Matthews said. "She probably got a lot of sympathy, 'oh, that poor woman. She's lost her daughter, her husband, all to this stomach flu.'"

Trueblood endured a brief but mandatory period of mourning after losing her family, but soon struck up a relationship with a waiter at her favorite Twin Falls restaurant. William McHaffie married Trueblood just two years after the loss of her first husband and only child, and the couple immediately sought an insurance policy for William. Trueblood was named as William's only beneficiary, to receive $5,000 if anything was to happen to him.

The couple moved to Hardin, Montana, and only a year after they married, William died of "influenza." According to his friends and customers, William had always been a robust, healthy man – and the speed and depth of his sudden illness shocked them.

"Lyda Trublood was very careful," said crime author Diane Fanning. "She waited until they actually got sick – then, it was easier to believe that they had died of an illness. Everybody thought it was something he ate that finally did him in, but all that it was, really, was Lyda Trueblood."

Unfortunately for Trueblood, however, William had failed to pay the second premium on his insurance policy, letting it lapse. Trueblood received nothing for her efforts. Days after her late husband's funeral, Trueblood sold all her property and disappeared.

Moving on

After relocating to Denver, Trueblood managed to ensnare another victim – a farm machinery salesman she had met during her previous marriage to William. In fact, William had told friends that after he'd come to their door in an attempt to make a sale, Trueblood had seemed "struck" by him – and neighbours reported that the happy couple had even started fighting more after that.

Trueblood married Harlan Lewis in March of 1919, and took him with her back to Montana. The couple settled in Billings, and only one month later, Harlan took out a $10,000 life insurance policy. According to Matthews, the larger policies are an indication that

Trueblood was manipulating the men in order to receive greater payouts.

"(Trueblood) was motivated by one thing, and one thing only - greed," said former FBI profiler Candice Delong. "She wanted money."

By mid-July, just three months after the wedding, disaster had struck. After falling ill to a sudden case "ptomaine poisoning," Harlan left Trueblood a widow for the third time – and this time, the cheque came through. After cashing out the estate, Trueblood disappeared again. Instead of heading somewhere new, however, Trueblood decided to return to Idaho.

Under the name of Lyda McHaffie, Trueblood checked into the Rogerson Hotel in Twin Falls in May 1919, and found herself a job at the Grille Café on Main Avenue. Business at the café picked up immediately, reports claim, and the foreman of Ira Perrine's Blue Lake Ranch, Edward Meyer, started visiting the restaurant regularly.

"Folks couldn't help noticing that the air sort of shimmered when (Trueblood's) eyes met Ed's," wrote Jaffe in his profile. "And that the ham he got was thicker, the eggs sunnier than those served other patrons."

The very next month, Trueblood moved to Pocatello, Idaho, where she married Edward Meyer and settled on a ranch.

"She rigged herself out fit to kill, bought a long mink coat and a closed car. Everybody in town was talking about the way she ran around to dances," said Ormsby. "She talked around town that she wasn't in love with Ed, but she wanted a home, and she said that sometime she might learn to love him."

Although she had started going by the name "Anna McHaffie," Trueblood showed no other signs of leaving her past life behind her. She applied for an insurance policy in Edward's name the day after the wedding, in the amount of $10,000 – however, the policy was not approved, and reasons were never clarified. It's possible that insurance companies were beginning to wise up to the run of bad luck Trueblood had encountered.

Suspicious situation

Only two weeks after the couple had wed, on August 25, Edward took ill. Doctors at the hospital claimed he had an excellent chance of recovery, but he was dead by September 7.

"She didn't wait for him to get sick," said Matthews. "Maybe she grew impatient, and that was probably the mistake she made in all of this."

Trueblood's previous husbands had been fairly low-key, unlikely to attract attention despite the unbelievable series of coincidences that had resulted in their deaths – and Trueblood's subsequent insurance claims. Edward Meyer, however, was a different case. As a prominent figure in Twin Falls, Edward had dealings with many of the leading business and farm people in the region – including the Twin Falls county sheriff.

"The townsfolk weren't just satisfied," Ormsby said. "They started a lot of talk, and the insurance company held up payment on the policy. The matter got into politics and folks wanted to know what the candidates for sheriff would do about (Trueblood)."

When traces of arsenic were discovered during a routine post-mortem examination, detectives finally brought the widow in for questioning.

"The investigation was just getting underway when the woman disappeared," stated an article published in the New York Times on May 13, 1921. "Detectives traced her to Los Angeles, and kept track of her while the bodies of the two (Dooleys), the infant daughter, and McHaffie were exhumed and portions of the viscera were sent to chemists."

Edward Meyer's death had become somewhat of a political issue in the 1920 campaign for sheriff, and potential candidates were asked how they planned to handle the case. The current sheriff passed the case to a "remarkable" deputy, Virgin Ormsby – and the investigation would be virtually his only assignment for months.

"After she left for California, the town got more dissatisfied than ever, and in January, I was assigned to the case," Ormsby said. "I've had the bodies of the men dissatisfied and examined – three chemists each working separately reported to me that they found arsenic. I interviewed the doctors who attended the husbands and obtained statements from them that enabled me to build a strong case against her."

Ormsby even discovered that a relative of Trueblood's first husband and brother-in-law had been studying the suspicious deaths in his family. A chemist named Earl Dooley had already begun to consider the possibility that Robert and Edward Dooley had been poisoned with arsenic – and according to Fanning, his suspicions led him to investigate the scene of Trueblood's most recent victim.

After taking samples from Edward Meyer's vomit in the sand, Earl had them tested.

"Sure enough, he found arsenic – and when that happened, he went to a doctor to get it confirmed in another lab," Fanning said. "It was definitely arsenic."

Mounting evidence

Police first determined that the Dooley brothers had been poisoned, as well as Trueblood's own child. Officers in Montana started investigating the cases of Harlan Lewis and William McHaffie, intrigued by the seemingly impossible coincidences that had led Trueblood to make so many insurance claims. Trueblood, meanwhile, was busy seducing her fifth husband, Paul Southard, in Los Angeles – while prosecutor Frank L. Stephen started building a case against her back in Twin Falls.

While working odd jobs, saving her money, and reportedly describing herself as a nurse, Trueblood managed to convince Paul to propose. The two were married in November of 1920. Although Paul, who served as a seaman in the navy, claimed he needed no additional insurance coverage beyond typical provisions, Ormsby learned that a policy had in fact been taken out on Chief Petty Officer Paul Southard – with Trueblood named as the beneficiary.

Shortly after they were wed, Paul was transferred from Los Angeles to Pearl Harbour, and his new bride joined him in Hawaii. Ormsby was in hot pursuit, having tracked Trueblood with the help of California law enforcement. Officers in Honolulu received a warrant for Trueblood's arrest in May 1921. She was picked up on May 12 to return to Boise, Idaho, for her trial – with her husband Paul at her side.

"She's been a mighty good wife to me," said Paul, who refused to believe the charges, "and I don't care if she married ten men before, and they all died. That wouldn't make her a murderess."

Although tabloids had already started running headlines about the gruesome tale, labelling Trueblood catchy names like "Lethal Lyda" or "The Arsenic Widow," Trueblood maintained her innocence as she and Paul prepared to catch the *Matsonia* out of Honolulu. Some reports claimed she was acting "like any lucky vacationer about to embark on an ocean cruise," her neck heavy with flowered leis.

"I am entirely innocent, and I look forward to the trip with optimism," Trueblood said in a brief statement to the press. "I am anxious to get back to Twin Falls and face my accusers."

At the jail, Trueblood finally granted an interview to reporter Hazel Pedlar Faulkner, with the San Francisco Examiner. Pedlar Faulkner described the accused as "dainty, friendly, and refined" – not exactly the picture of a "sinister murderer," she said.

"I have been nervous because of my imprisonment and the unnecessary disgrace to my husband," Pedlar Faulkner quotes Trueblood as saying. "I know as well as anything that I can clear myself. The evidence gathered against me is purely circumstantial. Their work is to prove the charges, and that will not be easy because of the documents I hold."

Trueblood claimed that her husbands had died because she was a "typhoid carrier," and even stated that she had nothing to do with the large life insurance policies her late husbands had all secured before their untimely deaths.

"Life insurance was no object to me," stated Trueblood in Pedlar Faulkner's interview. "I have had enough money. And what insurance my husbands carried were business propositions they took out without regard to me or without consulting me, generally."

Before leaving San Francisco to bring Trueblood back to Boise, Ormsby and his wife, Nellie, took the accused for one last night on the town. After having dinner at a restaurant and strolling through a downtown shopping district, the Ormsbys and their charge attended a vaudeville show at the Orpheum Theatre.

Although Trueblood was trying to remain under the radar, a San Francisco Chronicle reporter recognized her – and wrote about her activities the next morning.

"With the grim specters of four dead husbands, a brother-in-law, and her infant baby hovering near her, while the accusing finger of the law points at her and charges murder, Mrs. Lyda Eva Southard, psychological enigma, calmly spent yesterday seeing the sights of San Francisco," read Herb Westen's article in the San Francisco Call and Post.

"She smiles, a trifle shyly perhaps, but a bored light creeps around her eyes as if to her it is all a tedious legal jumble, which will steal precious hours from her pursuit of happiness."

Up to the jury

Despite Trueblood's denial of the charges, the state contended that she'd fed Edward Meyer, her fourth husband, hefty doses of arsenic extracted from flypaper. Trueblood denied it and the state presented further evidence – largely circumstantial, but it was still enough for a conviction.

The trial, which started on October 3 and lasted six weeks, received attention nation-wide. At the time, it would become the longest criminal trial in history. Witnesses were called from Missouri, Montana, Tennessee, and California – a total of 182 named to appear, but not all were called to the stand.

Prosecutor Stephen tried desperately to bring in Buddy Thornberg to testify against Trueblood – a reporter for the Daily News in Twin Falls who had come close to marrying Trueblood shortly before she snagged Edward Meyer. He'd met the widow at the café, and she had swept him off his feet. According to reports, Thornberg had told his friends he would be marrying the "rich widow from Montana," and – on her advice – he was considering taking out an additional private insurance policy on top of the $10,000 government policy he already had in place.

After his friends managed to convince him to not follow through with a marriage, however, Thornberg had ended his relationship with Trueblood and was presumed to have moved to Washington – never to be heard from again.

An article claimed that "every session of the trial found the court auditorium filled to capacity, principally by women and girls." Another report claimed the trail was, "draggy," and "rather technical – arsenic versus typhoid, laboratory tests versus the official death certificate. This certificate, giving typhoid as the cause of death, was more or less (Trueblood's) sole defense."

The whole case presented against Trueblood suggested that she didn't particularly love her husband, and could have – and likely did – poison him. Not only that, she took out insurance on his life, and fled immediately after his death.

According to Ormsby, a visit to the McHaffies' home in Montana had uncovered evidence to back up this theory. He'd discovered a "large quantity" of cut-up flypaper containing arsenic in the basement, with residue of arsenic in a pot Trueblood had likely used to boil the poison out – before serving it to her husband in tainted food.

"(Trueblood) went about her killing very deliberately," Fanning said. "She bought out everything the store had in flypaper. It was obvious that she wanted to have a permanent supply on hand."

An article published in the New York Times on October 9, 1921 stated that under the questioning of Prosecuting Attorney Frank Stephen, Dr E. F. Roberbaugh, state chemist, confirmed the presence of arsenic poison in the body of Edward Meyer when he examined the body in April of that year.

"The witness testified he found .05 milligrams of poison in five grams of a specimen of several internal organs and .10 milligrams in a ten-gram quantity of the specimen," the article read. "The witness said the distribution of poison throughout the system was not equal and he estimated that a little less than five grains of poison probably was contained in Meyer's body."

He added that the findings "virtually duplicated" those obtained immediately after Edward Meyer's death in September, 1920.

The state requested permission to introduce further evidence relating to the deaths of Trueblood's other husbands, and the judge ruled the testimony admissible. While physicians did, in some instances, contradict testimony of other expert witnesses on the question of cause of death, analysis made by three separate chemists agreed that poison was present in all bodies exhumed.

"She poisoned their food, and over time, the arsenic would build up," said Fanning. "Most of the death certificates all said some sort of stomach ailment."

After a deliberation of twenty-three hours, the jury came back with a verdict on November 4, 1921. Trueblood was found guilty of second-degree murder. Speculation was that the jury had "blanched" at the thought of hanging a woman, but there was no doubt that she had done it. Even her husband, Paul Southard, filed for divorce after watching the trial.

"Lyda Trueblood was a classic black widow," Delong said. "And she did it for money."

According to an article in the November 5, 1921 issue of the Sacramento Union, Trueblood showed "no sign of feeling," and didn't even raise her eyes from the floor as the verdict was read. This was typical of Trueblood's attitude throughout the trial, however.

"On the stand, the accused woman maintained an unperturbed attitude throughout a long grilling by the prosecution, which failed to adduce any important admissions from her," the article stated.

Only eight years after Trueblood's incarceration, Ormsby suffered a paralytic stroke and died in his wife's arms. His obituary ran on the front page of the December 30, 1929 edition of the Twin Falls Times – and flowers were delivered to his funeral, sent from a Lyda Southard.

A "break for freedom"

Still, the guilty verdict and the sentence of at least ten years in prison wasn't enough to keep Trueblood from seducing men.

"She proved that no prison walls can hold her, and made her escape from the Idaho State Penitentiary by fascinating, as did Milady, a prison guard, who is believed to have rigged up for her an ingenious ladder of plumbers' pipes and torn blankets and garden hose," read an article published in the October 25, 1931 issue of the Salt Lake Tribune. "This guard, however, died before (Trueblood) made her break for freedom."

According to the article, Trueblood had already served ten years of her sentence and was eligible for parole when she made her great escape on May 4, 1931. The ladder, fashioned for her by prison guard Jack Watkins, had been buried for months beneath the prison walls. Watkins had also provided Trueblood with a saw, which she used to remove a bar from her cell window.

"The escape itself was dramatic," the article continued. "Women inmates, evidently under the spell of the woman, who could fascinate those of her own sex as well as men, staged a party and played the phonograph and sang while she was gaining her way to liberty."

Trueblood ran right into the arms of David Minton. Minton, an ex-convict himself, had fallen under Trueblood's spell while he was still behind bars. After he helped Trueblood escape from prison, she'd ended the relationship. Leaving him alive was a mistake, however – enraged, Minton went to the police and told them they could find Trueblood in Topeka, Kansas.

This, however, was not before a nation-wide manhunt was organized to attempt to locate Trueblood, who was described by Warden R. E. Thomas of the Idaho State Penitentiary as "one of the most dangerous criminals at large."

"Some man will probably pay with his life in agony and death before this ruthless woman can again be brought to justice," he said. "That she is the modern 'Mrs. Bluebeard' is certain."

In fact, before the police found her in Kansas, Trueblood had managed to swindle another man into marrying her. Harry Whitlock, who later described Trueblood as a "model wife," was shocked when the police showed up looking for her. The relationship had begun when Trueblood, calling herself "Fern," had started doing housekeeping work for Whitlock – and she had suggested he take out a $20,000 life insurance policy, but it hadn't been purchased before she asked him for some travel money and took off.

Fifteen months after her escape, Trueblood was returned to Boise – with her marriage to Whitlock annulled.

Back in prison, Trueblood continued to seduce her prey. This time, she set her sights on George Rudd, a prison warden. She managed to convince him to grant her special privileges – frequent day trip to a local resort, visitation to see her sick mother, and even transportation to Boise to see movies. However, when authorities discovered that he'd been treating Trueblood to these privileges, Rudd was forced to resign from his position.

Free at last

Finally, Trueblood was paroled from prison on October 3, 1941, and fully pardoned only one year later.

"I think they figured that she had lost most of her good looks and charm, and was no longer a menace to society," Matthews said.

After spending a few years living with her sister, Blanche Quigley, in Nyssa, Oregon, Trueblood returned to her family's farm at Twin Falls – but the local townspeople and even her relatives weren't pleased to see her.

A few months later, Trueblood left for Provo, Utah, where no one knew her, and pulled together the funds to purchase a small secondhand shop. There, she married her seventh husband, Hal Shaw. However, once Shaw's children discovered who she was and learned about her unsavory past, he vanished – leaving her to move to Salt Lake City, where she worked for several years as a housekeeper and waitress.

"You wonder, did (the husbands) ever suspect that it was not a natural illness that was making them suffer in agony," Fanning said. "We can only hope that they never understood what was really happening."

Trueblood died of a heart attack on February 5, 1958 in Salt Lake City. Her body remains at Sunset Memorial Park in Twin Falls, Idaho, where she was buried as Anna E. Shaw. Still, some report seeing a ghost bearing Trueblood's likeness haunting the halls of the Idaho prison to this day – the prison's most notorious inmate, maintaining a presence even after her death.

"When she finally died, it was from a heart attack," Fanning said. "It's amazing to think that (Trueblood) actually had a heart."

BLACK WIDOW : THE TRUE STORY OF MARGARET RUDIN

114

BRIANNA VALDES

Margaret Rudin, dubbed the Black Widow of Las Vegas, went on trial on February 26, 2001 for the murder of her fifth husband, real estate king Ronald Rudin. After a lengthy, chaotic trial and her defense claiming that involvement in illegal activities resulted in Ron's death, the jury found her guilty on May 2, 2001. In August, the court sentenced Margaret Rudin to life in prison with the possibility of parole in 20 years.

According to reports, Ron Rudin went missing about a week before Christmas in '94. He paid a visit to wife Margaret Rudin's antique shop, in the same plaza as his real estate business. Officials said that Margaret Rudin did not report Ron missing until a few days after he disappeared. She told police she thought nothing of it at first because, aside from Ron being upset with her after an argument, he seemed like his usual self.

About a month after Ron disappeared, a couple of civilians stumbled upon human remain near Lake Mohave in Nevada. Police found ashes and fragments of bones in the burn pile. However, the skull, which was inches away, remained mostly intact. It had at least four bullet holes, which forensics later matched to a .22 caliber weapon. Police made two trips to the house, and on the second visit, they found blood on the walls, photographs and items removed from the house including a mattress and carpet. However, though the police suspected that Margaret Rudin killed her husband, the evidence up to that point was circumstantial at best.

A year and a half year later, a diver found a .22 caliber gun with a built-in silencer in Lake Mead. This was the same gun Ron Rudin reported missing about six years before his death. When officials tested the gun in the forensics lab, the ammo matched the rounds found in Ron Rudin's skull. Police determined that the .22 was the murder weapon, and, with this new piece of evidence added to the other circumstantial clues they had, charged Margaret Rudin with the murder of her husband. However, Margaret left town before they indicted and arrested her, and she stayed out of sight for over two years.

Almost a year after the diver found the gun that allegedly killed Ron Rudin, police finally indicted Margaret Rudin.

Authorities finally apprehended Margaret Rudin in 1999. Someone who saw her picture and story on the T.V. show "America's Most Wanted" called and reported seeing her in a small town in Massachusetts.

Police used a pizza delivery person to help them capture Margaret. They borrowed the person's uniform and an empty pizza box, and barged in the house when her male companion opened the door. According to some reports, they found her cowering in the bathroom.

Margaret Rudin was born Margaret Lee Frost in Memphis, Tennessee on May 31, 1943. She said that she and her family never lived in one place for very long, and that she and her two sisters constantly changed schools.

"I didn't grow up any place. We were constantly moving, you know, like, I transferred schools 22 different times, um, before I graduated high school. I lived in 15 states in 15 years. I never had a hometown."

Margaret said that her father was strict and dominating, and that he rarely showed affection to her or her sisters.

Both Margaret and Ron were married four times before they met at the First Church of Religious Science in Las Vegas. They married on September 11, 1987.

Margaret's mother, Eloise Frost, stood behind her daughter throughout the entire trial. She never believed Margaret capable of murder.

"I want to live long enough to see Margaret pronounced innocent, because she is innocent."

Margaret Rudin's daughter, Kristina Mason firmly believed that her mother was innocent. She said her childhood was a good one, and that the mother with whom she grew up was not a murderer.

"She's just a wonderful person and I'm proud to say she's my mother."

The court sentenced Margaret Rudin in September 2001. Although she received life in a medium security facility, plus a year for planting the bugs in her husband's office, they also added that she would be eligible for parole in 2011. She began preparing, and petitioning, for her appeal, carefully heeding the filing deadlines.

80-year-old Eloise cried when Margaret was convicted, saying that now she may never see her daughter again.

Kristina Mason burst into tears.

"I'm so disappointed."

Ronald Rudin seemed to predict his own death, or at least his murder. Months before he went missing, he had his will changed, with specific instructions for investigators to follow in the event that he died under suspicious circumstances.

"In the event my death is caused by violent means [for example gunshot, knife or a violent automobile accident] extraordinary steps be taken in investigating the true cause of the death. Should said death be caused directly or indirectly by a beneficiary of my estate, said beneficiary shall be totally excluded from my estate and/or any trusts I may have in existence."

Although most of Nevada's case against Margaret was circumstantial, authorities say there were a few things that seemed suspicious to them from the beginning. First, Margaret herself admitted that her marriage to Ron was less than ideal. She told police that they often argued about her work schedule. Later, when authorities discovered that she had planted listening devices in Ron Rudin's home office, she also admitted that she suspected that Ron was having an affair, and upon eavesdropping on a phone conversation, discovered proof to back her suspicions.

Jimmy Vacarro, a Vegas detective, confirmed that the Las Vegas police believed without a doubt that Margaret Rudin was responsible for Ron's murder.

"We know there was this real rocky roller-coaster relationship between Margaret Rudin and her husband... [It took] Margaret two days to file a missing persons report and that she did so only after Ron's coworkers informed police first...Generally speaking, the spouse is missing, the wife's the one reporting it."

Second, officials say that Margaret waited a few days before reporting Ron missing, even though his employees at his real estate company were concerned and investigating as soon as he did not show up that Monday morning.

Margaret Rudin offered a logical explanation to her hesitation to bring in police. She said she thought little of it at first because they had another fight and he left angry, which was common for Ron. She also said that, aside from Ron being upset with her after an argument, he seemed like his usual self.

"He seemed ok. He does not seem upset. He had, had been a little peeved at me over the weekend because I had to work all the time... "Well, I thought nothing of it because, you know, maybe he did get peeved... and maybe he did decide to go out for awhile... maybe he did go to, you know... wherever."

Margaret made a point of mentioning her previous marriages in one of her interviews.

"I don't have a history of staying with somebody if I'm really unhappy. I have a history of divorcing... There was problems. He was a difficult person at times, but yes, I did love him..."

Margaret said Ron also drank quite a bit after just a few months of marriage. However, she told reporters that she was not mad about the alcohol or the other women, even when Su Lyles, a close friend and a former employee of Mr. Rudin's, testified that in the fall of 1993, their relationship became more intimate. At least twice, she said, they had discussed their feelings for each other over the telephone during calls made from his office.

"You know why? It is because 99 percent of the men that I have ever had in my life had affairs. Ninety percent of men do, you might as well expect it."

Margaret admitted that, although the affairs wounded her, she loved her husband and desperately wanted to work out things with him.

Police grew even more suspicious when they discovered that Margaret hired a man named Augustine Lovato to help her remove some dirty carpet and furniture from the master bedroom. She then renovated the bedroom she shared with her husband into an office while Ron was still missing.

Lovato testified that the mattress and carpet he removed from the Rudin's home had suspicious brown stains on it and a strong odor that alarmed him.

"It didn't seem right, him still being missing and me turning their master bedroom into an office and then those splatters on that picture. Like I got the heebie-jeebies."

Lovato also claimed that he heard a strange sound in the bathtub in the master bathroom. He said that, upon inspection, it looked about the same color and consistency as the stains on the mattress and carpet he removed.

The same day he moved the allegedly bloodstained items from the Rudin's bedroom, Margaret Rudin asked Lovato to mail a package addressed to her mother. Lovato claimed that he forgot to mail the package, and ultimately turned it over to the police. After obtaining a search warrant, police opened the package and discovered several personal items inside, including a postcard from Israel signed "Love, Yehuda," a photo of Yehuda Sharon, the man with whom police suspected that Margaret Rudin was having an affair, and a handwritten letter from Rudin to her mother containing the message, "Please hold on to my Ye."

Attorneys discovered later that Lovato reported all these mysterious findings after Ron Rudin's other trustees announced their reward for information about Ron's disappearance. However, Lovato argued that he cooperated with police before anyone told him there was a reward, which Ron's trustees did grant him.

The most suspicious thing that Margaret Rudin did, according to police, was going on the run before the state served her with her indictment. Investigators believed that, if Margaret were innocent, she would not have fled. However, Margaret says that she ran out of fear, not guilt.

"[I ran] because I was afraid of being found by Ron's shadowy business associates... It was difficult. I was always looking over my shoulder. I was always afraid, I was afraid of who stood to gain the most, you know, from Ron's murder."

During the trial, the state also used the testimony of almost 70 witnesses, including Yehuda Sharon and Margaret's sister, Donna Cantrell. Prosecutors granted Yehuda Sharon total immunity in exchange for his testimony against Margaret Rudin. However, when he took the stand, he not only had little to say regarding Margaret's guilt, he denied aiding her in disposing of Ron Rudin's remains. He told the court that he rented a van, planning to make a trip from Vegas to California for his business on the night in question. However, he said that he only made it half way there and then turned around due to unexpected weather conditions. Furthermore, his destination was the opposite direction from the place where officials found Ron Rudin's remains. Once the prosecution determined that Margaret's friend, Yehuda Sharon, was likely not an accomplice to Ron's murder, no other suspects were detained or questions, and most people assumed that Margaret had somehow dismembered her husband's body, put it in the heavy steamer trunk and hauled it out to the desert all by herself.

Cantrell testified that she was aware of her sister's marital problems. She said that Margaret had spoken to her many times about Ron's drinking and her suspicions about his involvement with other women. She made comments on Rudin's restless desire to get away from Ron.

"I said, 'I thought you were going to divorce him,' and she said, 'He's not in very good health. He can't even walk without being out of breath, and I think I'll wait.' [Margaret told me] to tell [police] that she and Ron were getting along better than ever. And that the girlfriend wasn't an issue. [I don't] think that this statement would have been true."

Despite the authorities' strong belief that she murdered her husband, Margaret Rudin maintained her innocents. In interviews after the trial and her conviction, she states repeatedly that she loved her husband and could never kill him. She suggested that there might be another motive for her husband's murder.

"Nobody knows the whole Ron. That's the part that worries me. Maybe there's something that was going on with a business or a personal deal."

Margaret also suspected that someone knew more than they told detectives.

"I think that there are people that know things. I think that there are people who haven't come forth before. Maybe they didn't know how, maybe they were afraid, maybe they were intimidated."

Margaret Rudin's trial was rocky from the beginning. One of her defense attorneys, Michael Amador, started with an opening statement, which consisted of nothing but a long, irrelevant, self-based speech.

"This is a great day, in a lot of different ways. Some days are difficult; some days we hear bad news or we go through a difficult time, but every day, every day, depending on how you look at it, with a few exceptions, can be a celebration.

This is a great today for me. This is a culmination of a career. The people in this case, we are not strangers; we know each other. Chris and I were sworn in as deputy DAs the same day. And I congratulate Chris on a presentation that was organized and well thought out, the best money can buy. It was really good.

If you want to know an opinion about me, I guarantee you'll find some, different ones from different people. Not many people know me. I have few close friends, like Ronald Rudin had few close friends.

I could be a wonderful, caring father, coaching soccer, helping kids with their homework, which I did the first time I got married when they were young.

Then another day, I might scream at someone, yell at them for-I don't know-for asking me some question, because I was too busy and I was thinking of something else.

The difficulty I have at times is communicating to people. I have to look at it and talk to other people and they will bring me back down to earth and say, Mike, what are you trying to say? What are you trying to get across?"

Amador also made a strange, challenging statement.

"During the course of the trial, there may be objections and things like that. Don't worry about it."

Judge Joseph Bonaventure cut off Amador's speech.

"I don't know what that means: Don't worry about objections. We have to do other things. I have no idea what that means. If there's an objection, I'm either going to overrule it or sustain it and that's the law...

I keep saying this-and I let you get away with a lot, Mr. Amador-but the purpose for an opening statement is just to indicate what the evidence is going to tend to show and not go into your personal beliefs and your passion and soccer dad and yelling at the staff and whether you were a green lawyer and know all the cops and used to be a D.A. and you communicate differently. I never heard that in [an] opening statement in my life."

During the opening statements, the State quoted a portion of Margaret Rudin's diary.

"My life has always been unique, exciting, full of change, challenges and stimulus and full of interesting casts of characters and that is okay.

It just is, and I accept that for my past, but I know that, by programming my mind, I can now redirect any future stage plays and pick my own screen play and cast, because I am the producer, director and star of any and all new plays on my stage called life.

I've always vaguely known these facts and lived my life accordingly, but I never realized what control-I never realized what control I could have over every segment of this one time stage production called "Margaret's Life.""

Amador did a curious thing at the trial. He employed a makeup artist from a professional modeling agency and paid almost $500 an hour, out of his own pocket, to make Margaret appear worn, delicate, and tired.

Amador got under Judge Bonaventure's skin by repeatedly being late to appear in court, questionable forms he submitted, and his cell phone, which he never turned off or down during the trial. Rumors eventually spread that Amador was using drugs, drinking and partying all night long when he had to be in court early the next morning.

Rumors circulated that Amador was also behaving inappropriately with Margaret Rudin's belongings and private, confidential information. Amador hired a new office assistant named Annie Jackson during the proceedings for the Rudin trial. She revealed information regarding some of the rumors about Amador.

"There is no other way to say the following: when Mr. Amador told the court that he did not have any book or movie contracts, he was lying. Michael Amador does have book contracts and movie contracts regarding the Margaret Rudin case. When we returned to the office after Mr. Amador made those false representations to the court, he asked me to grab all of the contracts so that he could put them in his little safe in the back closet. He told me, "I don't want anyone to find out that I have these, then I'm sure they'll be investigating and looking for these.""

Margaret asked early on for an even amount of participation from her attorneys. She asked that Thomas Pitaro take a more active role in the proceedings, because she did not believe that Michael Amador was properly prepared.

"We haven't even subpoenaed my witnesses yet. And I'm getting so nervous. I mean, I'm getting panicky."

Pitaro agreed after warning the judge that, although he would do his best, he was uncertain if he would be able to uphold that bargain throughout the entire trial.

Throughout all the chaos in the Rudin trial, one juror believed Margaret's side of the story. During the first couple of days of deliberation, she held fast to her opinion that Margaret did not kill Ron. However, hours before the foreperson read the jury's verdict, juror #11 changed her vote. She was distraught, wiping her eyes with a napkin. She hesitated before replying with a hushed "Yes" when the court asked her if the verdict was, in fact, hers, too.

Even though the verdict was ultimately unanimous, the juror cried as she apologized to Rudin when the foreperson read the jury's verdict.

During the time before she opted to vote Margaret Rudin guilty, juror #11 faced allegations from her peers of choosing not to join the deliberation efforts, lying, and calling one of the jury substitutes with her concerns about the case. Amador said he thought the juror was possibly "brow-beaten" into changing her vote.

Foreperson for the Rudin case's jury, Ronald Vest, said that no one "twisted her arm."

"We didn't bribe her or threaten her. She came to this on her own."

Vest believed that Rudin's was an open and shut case.

"Rudin's guilt was clear early on. [The defense's case was] a waste of time... [Amador was] bordering on incompetent... [The guilty verdict was a] slam dunk with a stepladder... I didn't buy any of it. I don't think any of us bought any of the defense case. The mountain of evidence had 11 of the jurors ready to convict as early as Thursday, but one person from the beginning did not see it that way... juror #11 seemed so bent on acquitting Rudin that [I] began to wonder if she had been bribed or threatened or simply wanted attention. [I] confronted her about [my] suspicions, and she denied them. There was a little bit of swearing. It was fast and furious but we hashed it out."

Vest admitted that he had had to request substitutes on a few occasions, because his special needs students were struggling in class without him. He believed that, had he not been there, they would not have been able to replace him.

"Six substitutes, three of which said they would never come back and one who just sat at the desk shaking like he was scared... my principal said, Well, maybe there's some reason why you need to be on this jury."

The judge in the Rudin trial met with the hesitant juror privately, in his chambers, to address her contact, and discussion about case-related information, with an alternate juror. Whenever Margaret Rudin's defense team broached the subject, the court dismissed it, stating that it had little impact on the outcome of the trial.

Margaret Rudin's conviction shocked Amador. He spoke with disdain about the prosecutors. He could not believe that the prosecutors successfully sold their case.

"If you have any understanding of psychology, history, or criminology, women don't do that, men do," said Amador. "That kind of mutilation is done by men over money or, in rare cases, serial killers. Women don't even order stuff like that—they want it clean... [The prosecutors] make me sick... I don't know how it is that right-thinking people can find someone guilty with no evidence."

Rudin had requested a mistrial due to Amador's antics and all the dissention with the jury. Pitaro led the defense team at the motion, hoping to prove that Amador was ill prepared for the case and not behaving with appropriate competence as an attorney.

"The fundamental problem that we have is this case is not ready to go to trial. For whatever reason it's not ready, it's not ready. That's obvious to any observer of this case, that for the first two weeks this is not the way you try cases and this is not the way you try murder cases. And what we are putting on in front of the world is a farce, and that disturbs me as an attorney. [T]his has become a sham, a farce and a mockery."

The State expressed similar concerns.

"Already we have an appellate issue now, should they have hired a forensic accountant. And I mean they came into this thing hiring their experts two weeks before the trial and they didn't start looking at the evidence until the day of trial. Two days into it, we still don't have reports back for most of them... Mr. Pitaro is coming in now, he's going to try to read the stuff and catch up. He already feels there's certain things that should have happened that didn't happen. All I can say is we're really uncomfortable with the record here."

The district court, however, was hesitant to declare a mistrial because of the double jeopardy laws. As it turned out, those did not apply in Margaret Rudin's case.

Amador stood with Margaret Rudin and the rest of her defense team during the motion for mistrial. However, when the prosecutors submitted documentation regarding his ineffectiveness, he contradicted himself.

"Nobody worked harder or spent more time before or during the Rudin trial nor knew the case better than I... [I] spend many hours on the case, from the time [I] took it in August of 2000 and [my] vacation in November 2000... [I] filed at least 24 motions and investigated all major witnesses in the case and organized their files prior to the vacation."

The defense also argued that improper communication took place between the judge, juror 11 and the alternate, which tainted the jury. According to the alternate, juror 11 called the alternate, saying she was upset because she was the only person in favor of a not guilty verdict and because she had gotten into an altercation with the staff person at a restaurant during a recess. After questioning the alternate and the juror in the presence of the State and the defense, the district court denied Rudin's motion for a mistrial. The district court also chose not to replace the juror. They concluded that neither the jury nor Rudin's case were compromised.

The court removed Amador from Margaret Rudin's case, but rejected her request for a mistrial. The judge almost immediately disregarded Margaret's mistrial motion.

"[Rudin] failed to present any specific argument to support a determination that she has been prejudiced. [The] affidavits are legally insufficient, as conclusions, rumors, beliefs, and opinions are not sufficient to form a basis for a new trial... As to Mr. Amador's personal antics which the defense seems to harp upon as tantalizing tidbits, this court feels it is not honorable to kick a man when he is down as the record speaks for itself. Rudin, at taxpayer expense, also had at her side criminal defense attorneys Thomas Pitaro and John Momot."

Bonaventure was biased, blunt, and cold at Margaret's sentencing hearing, just as he was throughout the entire trial.

"You're going to be locked away in the cold confines of your prison cell, never to be heard from again."

Although she received life in a medium security facility, plus a year for planting the bugs in her husband's office, they also added that she would be eligible for parole in 2011. She began preparing, and petitioning, for her appeal, carefully heeding the filing deadlines.

The appeals court believed that one of Margaret Rudin's former attorneys, Dayvid Figler, was responsible for her initial petitions for appeal. Figler denied any wrongdoing, and said that, although he was not at fault, she did deserve a shot at a new trial.

"I didn't screw up her trial. I didn't screw up her appeal. The court was giving extra time to get this very burdensome case before it. Everyone was operating under the assumption that she had more time to file the post-conviction appeal."

Figler called Rudin's appeal a "very complicated, burdensome, voluminous case" and said that after he took it on, the trial judge granted him extra time because the case was so complex.

Christopher Oram, the lawyer who represented Margaret Rudin during her recent appeal for a new trial, was thrilled with the opportunity.

"She is absolutely innocent. We've been working to prove it for a long time. I'm trying to reverse 10 years of complex litigation that was very unfair... I believe in her innocence. I'm ready to fight, and I wish they would stop playing their games. In the end, get in the ring and fight."

The Ninth Circuit Court of Appeals said that a technicality should not hinder Margaret Rudin's attempt to prove that a lawyer at her original trial ineffectually proved her case. Judge Mary Murguia believed that Figler did not serve Margaret to the best of his ability.

"While Figler regularly attended the court's status hearings, he appears to have done nothing else in support of his client's request for post-conviction relief. [Figler had the case for 645 days] and during that time, [he] had filed nothing in either state or federal court."

In 2007, Oram filed the first and only petition for post-conviction relief, according to Murguia.

Sally Loehrer, a district judge, ruled in 2008 that Michael Amador's performance did constitute as ineffectual in her original trial, and as a result, Margaret Rudin was entitled to a new trial.

"[It was a] case laced with intrigue and spins and loops involving a cast of characters and witnesses [that seemed to have] a lot of ulterior motives."

However, two years later, the Supreme Court overruled, stating that there was not enough evidence to sustain the order.

The Ninth Circuit Court reviewed all the evidence from the original trial, as well as Margaret Rudin's complaints, and her defense team's strategies. They do not believe that all defense attorneys adequately represent their clients just because they participate in every aspect of the trial. They made mention of evidence that was not previously mentioned.

"Sometime during the trial, the defense team located the person who sold the trunk to Rudin and established that it was not a large humpback trunk, but one that was much too small to fit a corpse inside. The defense also located Barbara Orcutt, who indicated that Rudin was indeed concerned about Ron's disappearance and had asked her right after his disappearance to organize a search in the Mt. Charleston area, where she believed Ron might have been. The State apparently had this information, but did not share it with the defense. It is unrealistic to think that the jurors could have put out of their minds all the evidence and adverse events, including the continual admonishment of defense counsel by the district court judge; the bizarre opening statement; the constant continuances and delays throughout the trial, which I am sure were held against the defense; and the belated presentation of important evidence. These harmful events resulted from Amador's conflict of interest and lack of preparation and now require reversal of this case... The evidence certainly indicated that Amador secured media rights while representing Rudin, which was a violation of the Nevada Rules of Professional Conduct.9...Amador was clearly more interested in obtaining information for his book and getting media attention than in developing Rudin's defense."

They also noted the testimony from Annie Jackson, Amador's assistant, and found new information there, as well. Jackson claimed that Amador did not turn over several of Rudin's files, containing diaries, witness statements, and pictures, to the public defender's office because he thought he might need the information in the future.

"I believe there is sufficient evidence in the record, without the necessity of post-trial proceedings, to establish that the defense was totally unprepared to try this case and that Amador had a substantial conflict of interest with his client. This was prejudicial to Rudin, and the result reached was unreliable."

Margaret appeals to the public in a letter she wrote from the Florence McClure Women's Correctional Center.

"The new trial I won [on] March 10, 2015, in the Ninth Circuit Court of Appeals has been blocked by the new NV Attorney General. Next week, their writ to the U.S. Supreme court will be filed."

She explains that, if her case lands in the 99% that skip review this session, it will return to the Ninth Circuit. Since they have already voted in her favor before, she hopes that once again, the NCCA will find her worthy of a new trial, and that this time their decision will be permanent. She maintains her innocence, and she continues to push for her appeal, and her opportunity to have her side of the story told.

HUSBAND KILLER MICHELLE REYNOLDS

131

GARY GUIDEN

On July 5th, 2004, a Frito Lay delivery pulled into the empty parking lot of a distribution center in Rome, Georgia. The man noticed that another man- one he didn't recognize- was coming out of the office, and although someone in the office in the early morning hours wasn't unusual, not recognizing the man was. According to the diver, the man who came into view appeared to be nervous- looking over his shoulder, glancing around, and checking behind him.

The man, possibly unaware of the delivery driver still sitting in his vehicle, exits the building and enters a mini-van after removing his shirt. Thinking this was odd, the delivery driver entered the Frito Lay office only to discover the scene of a horror film.

He discovered the slumped over body of the regional manager, Thad Reynolds, sitting in a pool of his own blood. He called 911 and EMT's and police officers responded within minutes. However, it was too late. Thad Reynolds was dead before anyone arrived.

Ross Cavitt, a reporter at the scene, noted that Reynolds had been stabbed 19 times. Due to the nature of the stab wounds and the amount of blood, it was obvious to Cavitt that there had been a great struggle.

Thad's death sent shock through his community, but hit his church, the Hollywood Baptist, the hardest as Thad and his wife Michelle were well-known within the church community. In her early days, Michelle had been popular in high school and well respected within her community.

Thad, on the other hand, was a dedicated Christian and devoted father to his 4 children, as well as a loving husband to his wife, Michelle. As a young man, Thad had been heavily involved in sports and was popular at his high school.

"He could always make your day better" stated Julie Crumbley about her late friend Thad.

Michelle was a mother of 4 and a likeable person, according to Thad's close friend, Julie Crumbley.

Before becoming a mother, Michelle had worked as an administrative assistant, but had given the job up after giving birth to her first child in 1992. After the couple began to have children, the decision was made that Michelle would be a stay at home mom and raise their children.

In 1995, however, the couple's relationship took a turn for the worse and Michelle asked for a divorce. Thad's sister, Beverly Owners, claims that Michelle hadn't been happy just being a mother and a wife. It's been said that Michelle had made the following comment to a pastor at the couple's church: "You put your wife on a pedestal, but Thad never put me on a pedestal."

Thad agreed to the divorce, but regretted his decision as he didn't believe in divorce or broken homes. Undone by the divorce, Thad turned to his church for help. Two years after their divorce, the couple remarried, built a new home, and added more children to their family.

Thad's career began to flourish, after he was hired into the Frito Lay company where he was able to work his way to district manager. He also sang in the church's choir and served as a deacon, as well as helped other couples with marriage counseling.

"They appeared to be the most perfect family whenever you would see them" says Crumbley.

Thad's mother told Dateline that the couple had been called Barbie and Ken because of how well their life seemed to be going.

Both Michelle and Thad had a passion for children and worked with the church's youth group to put on shows, skits, and performances in various locations. They worked closely with the church's youth minister, Scott Harper and his wife, Paige. Thad and Scott became best friends and the families became joined at the hip. Paige and Michelle also became close, bonding over their stay at home lifestyles and busy husbands.

So, what went wrong? The answer to this was revealed only after a shocking truth involving Michelle and her best friend's husband came to light.

In 2004, Thad decided to become a minister, as he felt that God was calling to him to join the ministry. In June of that year, Michelle signed up to help the Harper family with a youth retreat, but called Paige shortly before they were set to leave and said that she had had a change of heart.

"She called me last minute and said that she was going to book her own room and was not going to room with me, because she needed her own time" says Paige, when asked about the phone call. This meant that Michelle would be the only chaperon who had her own private room.

"Michelle was distant. She wouldn't speak to me or look me in the eye" Paige says. Paige grew concerned and confronted her best friend. "I said "Michelle is there something wrong? Have I done something to offend you?" and she looked me in the eye and said no, I just want to be around people who are on fire for God."

As her husband prepared to become a minister, Michelle began to spend less time with Paige and more time with her husband, Scott.

"She would constantly be asking him for assistance. More and more she would ask him for help working with the children or how to do certain things with them. They began to email and communicate" says prosecutor, Leigh Patterson.

On Saturday, July 3rd, 2004, the Harper and Reynolds' met up for a long weekend celebration. The next day, a Sunday, the met up once again to attend church together. That day, the families met at a local park to play volleyball, gave snacks, and enjoy each other's company.

"I noticed Michelle being kind of flirtatious towards other men, asking somebody to help her throw a football and stuff like that." Paige says.

"She was a little bit too flirty...wanting other men to pay attention to her" agrees Patterson.

Despite Michelle's odd behavior at the picnic, she and her husband loaded up their children at the end of the evening and went home like nothing had happened.

The next morning Thad left for work before sunrise and while Michelle and the kids were still asleep. After only a few minutes at the office, a van pulled up outside of the office where Thad was working. The driver was Scott Harper, and within a few minutes, Thad would be dead on the floor of his office.

On July 5th, when Thad's body was discovered, the city of Rome, Georgia was thrown into chaos.

The first question on investigator's lips was who would launch a violent attack on the well-loved church deacon?

"There were wounds all over his body, including defensive wounds" says Patterson.

The only witness had been the delivery driver who had discovered Thad's body, but he had been unable to get a good look at Thad's attacker's face or the license plate of the van he had been driving.

Upon investigation of the scene, it became apparent to police that Thad had managed to wound his attacker. This was proved by a large amount of blood that was found by the office doorway- blood that matched up with the delivery driver's statement claiming that the unknown man stopped by the door before getting into his van and leaving the scene.

Also on the scene, police found the empty case for a hunting knife and a pair of glasses. The glasses also matched up with witness testimony, as the man was seen removing his shirt and in doing so, his glasses could have fallen off and been left behind in his haste to get away.

Scott Harper was called to help identify Thad's body and was one of the first people to learn of his death. Scott called his wife and upon hearing the news, Paige become worried about Michelle.

The Harpers drove to the Reynolds house to be with Michelle, however, upon arrival, they found that the church's head pastor was already there.

According to family and friends, Michelle has taken the news stoically.

"You would think that when we got there, Michelle would come and give us a hug or cry and she didn't" said Beverly Owens, surprised at how Michelle took the news.

Thad's mother also noticed Michelle's lack of outward emotion and was concerned by it.

"She had just bought a black dress about two weeks before and made the comment "whoever thought that I'd be using it for this.""

Meanwhile, back at the crime scene, investigators had begun to wonder about Thad's death. To them, it didn't appear to be a random attack and robbery situation, but seemed to have been calculated and planned, as Thad's murderer didn't take any of his money or anything that he had had on him. The reason behind the attack appeared to be one thing: to kill Thad Reynolds.

On the news that evening, a clue was unearthed as to who could have killed the deacon. Scott Roberts, a coworker of Scott Harper, had heard the news asking for leads and picked up the phone almost immediately.

Roberts called the police department and reported to the officials that his coworker, Scott Harper was both friends with Thad and drove a burgundy minivan like the one that had been witnessed leaving the crime scene.

Roberts was asked for a statement and while telling them what he knew, he alerted the police that Scott Harper had been having an affair with someone- information that he claimed he had stumbled upon without meaning to. Roberts worked with phonelines and was tasked with fixing them. A few weeks before the murder, he had tapped into a conversation to fix the phoneline and overheard Harper talking to a woman who wasn't his wife, Paige. He had also overheard that the woman's name was Michelle.

"They were flirting. Lover chit chat, if you will. Kind of reminded me of high school sweethearts" said Roberts in an interview with Dateline.

Officials ended their interview with Roberts by asking a simple question- did Harper wear glasses? Roberts had answered that, yes, Scott Harper did wear glasses.

This left police to wonder were the connections between the van, the glasses, and a possible affair all just coincidence? Or was there something sinister going on?

The Harpers were then brought in for official questioning, where Scott told investigators that he had hurt his hand at the gym, when he was asked why his hand was bandaged. This explained his hand but didn't explain why his glasses were missing.

Scott was released, despite police not believing his story. Paige was starting to doubt her husband, as well.

"When we left the station, I asked him if he knew anything about Thad's murder...about what was going on" Paige said "and he said "do you realize what you're asking me?""

Police obtained a warrant to search Scott's computer at the hospital that he worked at, in hopes of getting answers. They had a particular interest to look into Scott's emails, as they were saved on a public server and could be easily accessed.

It was found that a large portion of the emails were to and from Thad's wife, Michelle. At first, the emails were innocent- mostly consisting of routine topics such as the youth group that Michelle worked with at the church. Gradually, though, the emails became more personal and revealing in nature.

About a month before the death of her husband, the tone of the emails changed.

"She was coming onto him in the emails. Usually under the guise of I know I shouldn't feel this way" Patterson says, referring to Michelle and the emails that she sent to Scott "and he fell for it."

"The emails, especially toward the end, were very graphic and specific" said prosecutor Natalee Staats.

It wasn't clear from the emails when their affair became physical, however, records show that at the youth retreat in June, Scott had booked Michelle's room and stayed in it with her. Paige, although quiet about the whole thing, had noticed Scott get up and leave the room and noted that he didn't return until the next morning.

"He had gone down to Michelle's room and even though they were on a church trip with kids and his wife, and Michelle's daughter there as a participant, they had continued their affair" said Patterson.

Police combed over every detail of their emails, but couldn't decide whether Michelle had coaxed Scott into murdering her husband or not. According to Patterson, Michelle had been very careful with what she said and how she said it.

"Michelle never said "I need you to kill my husband" said Staats. However, she hinted at the idea by sayings things like "You'll have to live longer than Thad for us to be together because he'll never agree to divorce."

After Michelle had planted the idea in Scott's head, he had gone on to lookup poison and arsenic, as well an essay on how to commit the perfect murder Patterson reported.

On the evening of July 4th, hours before the murder would happen, the two exchanged a final round of emails.

"The night before, she tells him what Thad's schedule was going to be the next morning. Specific directions of where he was going to be" she also reports.

"Those were all glaring clues to the police that Michelle might have been involved in a conspiracy to murder her husband" said Staats, in agreeance with Patterson.

Scott had sent Michelle an email giving her an out. The email told Michelle to tell him if she had any hesitations, and that if she did, he wouldn't go through with it. Michelle replied that didn't have any hesitations and was ready for the event to take place.

Scott Harper was charged with murder on July 8th, 2004 after he turned himself in. He was charged with murder, felony murder, aggravated assault, and aggravated battery.

Authorities hoped that Scott would tie Michelle into the case, however, Scott was blinded by his feelings for her and was willing to protect her at all costs. He invoked the right to remain silent and didn't make another statement for or against Michelle's innocence.

Michelle was also arrested, as police had enough evidence from Michelle's own emails, that she had been involved.

"Once they figured it out, they decided pretty quickly that they had enough to charge her as well" said Michelle's attorney, Jim Berry.

An hour or so after Scott had turned himself in, Michelle was placed under arrest and brought into police custody and like her lover, Michelle refused to talk.

"Michelle was arrested as she came out of her attorney's office in downtown Rome" said Patterson.

"I had no clue. Everybody seemed happy" said Paige, who was shocked by the news that Michelle and Scott were in custody.

"Friends that they interacted with at the church didn't dream that the family pastor was having an affair with the deacon's wife" Patterson said.

The fact that Michelle and Scott could and would conspire to murder Thad Reynolds was unthinkable to the members of the church, who knew both people as being kind and good-hearted.

Scott Roberts, after hearing the news, took it upon himself to search the hospital where he and Scott worked for anything that police might have missed. He focused on the IT department's data center and more specifically, he focused on the tile floor. He was able to lift up a tile using a suction cup, and underneath, found the item that would be pinned as the murder weapon: a hunting knife. He also discovered a pile of bloody clothes.

In November, 4 months after Thad's murder, Michelle and Scott were summoned to the court room for a preliminary hearing to decide who would be tried first.

"The state gets to elect, by law, who to try first. We had elected to try her first" said Patterson. The decision to try Michelle first was a risk, as her case was the weaker of the two. Prosecutors knew that she hadn't bene the one to physically take Thad's life, however, they held her responsible for the murder.

"She was the person that made it happen" said Ross Cavitt "even though Scott Harper had the murder weapon in his hand, they could see that he was following orders from Michelle which made her ultimately responsible for the crime."

The emails, although suspicious, didn't pin Michelle to giving the orders, but prosecutors hoped that Harper would. They hoped that by presenting him with the evidence that was quickly stacking against him, they would be able to convince him to cut a deal and turn his back on Michelle.

Aside from the leverage of evidence that prosecutors had, the DA had written and notified the court that she would be seeking the death penalty for both Scott and Michelle.

"After the death of a fine young man, a father of four, to seek the death penalty wasn't that surprising" said Cavitt, in regard to the DA's email.

All that was left for prosecutors to do was wait and hope that Scott would cave.

"I had begged Scotty to do what was needed and to give up the information, and to tell the story of his involvement and Michelle's involvement" Paige told Dateline "and he would always tell me no, to just leave her out of this"

"He was smitten and head over heels in love with her" Cavitt said.

"I think that she couldn't have cared less about him. I think he was just the muscle behind the act" said Patterson, who was convinced that Michelle had simply used Harper's infatuation with her to get him to do her bidding.

Despite the prosecutor's hopes, Harper continued to clam up when it came to Michelle's involvement. It seemed that even the threat of the death penalty wasn't enough to get him to talk.

Years passed this way.

"Meetings with him resulted in nothing. He would not come forward" said Staats.

Finally, in the fall of 2008 and 4 years after both parties had been locked behind bars, Scott was ready to cooperate with prosecutors.

Scott's attorneys helped him decide on a deal and upon this conversation, it became to clear to everyone involved that Harper was still infatuated with Michelle as his concern for her took center stage. He would take a life sentence and plead guilty, as long as the death penalty was taken off of Michelle's case. He did, however, agree to testify at Michelle's trial.

"He effectively saved and betrayed her at the same time" said one of his attorneys.

In the court room on October 1st, 2008, Harper sat with prosecutors and told them his account of Thad's death.

"He told us that he still loved her and he was going to do anything in his power to minimize her involvement" said Patterson

"Michelle had basically said that Thad would not leave easily. He would fight for her and not give up on their marriage and that it would get ugly" said another of his attorneys "and he said that he could deal with ugly."

After this conversation, according to Scott, he had purchased the hunting knife and the next day, he had had lunch with Michelle. The two had parked and kissed in the back seat like a pair of teenagers, and it was during this time that Michelle had asked him if he had talked to her husband yet. When he told her that he hadn't, Michelle withdrew her affection and became cold and distant towards him.

Scott said that he had been afraid of losing her, so four days later he had woken up before dawn and driven to the Frito Lay distribution center with the intent to deal with Thad Reynolds.

As he entered the building, Thad had looked up and asked him what he was doing there. Scott Harper had replied with "I want what you got."

Harper's story was not enough to pin the murder on Michelle: it was only enough to charge her with adultery.

"All it would take was for one person on the jury to say that okay. Maybe Michelle really did think that Scott was just going to talk to her husband" Patterson said.

On January 13th, 2010, Michelle was brought back into court after 6 years of being in jail. The officials and attorneys present had been expecting for Harper to testify against Michelle, however, this did not happen. Michelle stood before the jury and plead guilty to voluntary manslaughter.

"Getting Scott Harper's statement was like pulling teeth and she didn't think we'd get it. That's the only reason that she plead guilty"

" She knew that she was responsible for the death, in some way, because of the affair and because of that she felt that she should plead guilty to something" said Scott's attorney.

At the hearing that day, Thad's mother asked Michelle why her son had had to die for this.

"There was no response" said Thad's mother, Kittie Walker, "her eyes were just cold. No remorse, no feelings, nothing."

"She knew that Thad would not have let her take the kids away" said Beverly Owens "and she knew that that was the only way to get him out of the picture"

In the end, she was sentenced to 20 years behind bars, with credit being given to the time she had already served in county jail. Until her release, Michelle is unable to see her children and will lose custody of them.

According to Scott Roberts, there were people who upon hearing her sentencing, didn't feel as if justice had been served.

"I would have liked to see Michelle get a lot more time for it. I would have liked to see her life in prison" said Kittie Walker.

Many people in Rome, Georgia agreed that although Scott had wielded the knife, Michelle was the villain behind the plot.

"We're in a religious town and I think that many people believed that Scotty had been manipulated by her and that she was the devil incarnate" said Jim Berry.

Despite the tension and hard feelings, Paige Harper was visibly shaken by the case.

"Scott and Michelle were the two most important people in my life other than my kids, so for this to happen...it really makes me wonder how well I know people" she said.

In the aftermath of the murder, Thad's mother got custody of the kids and Paige divorced her husband in 2005. Despite writing letters in the early days of their sentences, Michelle and Scott have stopped communicating.

Within recent years, Michelle has written to officials asking why she isn't allowed to see her children.

"We do it all the time with adults- no contact with whomever. That's not anything new. That's a standard law order in nearly every murder case I've had, even if they're in the same family" responded Patterson, who also stated that Michelle is well aware of this order as it was part of her plea deal back in January of 2010.

Judge J. Bryant Durham, who had found Michelle guilty in years prior, mentioned that once her children turn 18 they can visit her in prison. Currently, this means that Michelle's eldest daughter, 22-year old Alisan and her infant grandchild can visit her in prison whenever they wish.

"Like it or not, if she decides to go over there every day, I don't think that can be stopped" Durham told Patterson.

The intent of the order was to restrict visitation until Michelle was released, however, due to lack of specifics and bad wording, the age of visitation remains 18.

There's no question that a good man died for less than good reasons, but there are still questions in the minds of his family and friends. Why had it happened? Had death really been Michelle's only option? It's up for speculation and, unfortunately, no one will ever know for sure.

HUSBAND KILLER : THE TRUE STORY OF MICHELLE HALL

145

TORI BAKER

It's never easy being a member of a blended family. There's a certain understanding that comes along with a second or third marriage – especially one involving children – that there is going to be a fundamental need for combined effort, tolerance and compromise.

When Michelle Garner remarried for what would be the third and last time, family and friends believed she had finally found happiness after reconnecting with an old high-school flame.

John Brittson "Britt" Hall, an aircraft mechanic and home builder, had known his own fair share of heartache; he was recently divorced when he found his old high school girlfriend, Michelle, on an online dating web site.

Britt Hall and Michelle Garner first met in 1986 while attending high school in Newnan, GA. The two briefly dated before Michelle Hall graduated in 1987.

"They both were in the popular clique," forensic psychologist Robert Brion said. "Britt was a baseball player that all of the girls had a crush on. Michelle was popular herself, very outgoing with a lot of friends."

The parents of Britt and Michelle were friends as well but they didn't consider the dating relationship between Michelle and Britt to be a serious one. After graduation, Michelle would move away and she would marry a man named Rusty Hart. The couple would have two daughters until their divorce in 1996.

The single mom worked as a dental assistant to support her daughters. Times were tight until 1999 when she met and married Steve Davis.

"Steve Davis was a businessman," Brion said. "He was divorced himself with a daughter of his own. He met Michelle and quickly fell for her charms as she could come across as a very warm and caring person. He asked her to marry him after about a year of dating."

Michelle would become pregnant during the union and give birth to her third daughter, Alyssa.

Unfortunately, her second marriage met the same fate as her first and within a few years, the couple had filed for divorce, citing irreconcilable differences.

Britt did well for himself after high school, becoming an airline mechanic for Delta Airlines. He made good money with Delta until they laid him off. He then went into business with his father in home construction until ultimately returning back to Delta after they had a rehire.

His marriage started to fail, however. His first wife cited that Britt had "mental problems" and filed for divorce, stating that the marriage was "irretrievably broken."

"Britt's first wife would take him to court at least six to eight times a year after their divorce," Brion said. "He was depressed and the court visits weren't helping."

His divorce would coincide with Michelle's impending divorce with Steve Davis. Her divorce with Davis was a particularly nasty one and Britt could sympathize. They would reconnect over a dating website.

In the midst of her own divorce, Garner was happy to find love again with Britt Hall as they rekindled old flames. Shortly after reconnecting, Britt invited Michelle over for Sunday lunch with his family, and all seemed well for the couple.

"Michelle did mention to Britt's family that she was going through some difficult times with her divorce," Brion said. "She was cheerful throughout but hinted that the custody battles she was going through were quite serious."

Little did Britt Hall's family know that their excitement would soon be turned to devastation; a tragedy that would make national headlines and be detailed in various murder documentaries.

THE BRADY BUNCH

Ronald Hall, Britt's father was all to happy to have Michelle back in his son's life. At least at first.

"We visited and talked," Ronald said. "And she came in and was just as happy as she ever was," he said.

It wasn't long before Britt Hall's romance with Garner turned more serious, and the two tied the knot in September of 2006. The new marriage was an adjustment, to say the least. Britt had three children from his previous marriage and Michelle Hall had three of her own children as well. The blended family of eight was now living in Britt Hall's town home.

"You can imagine how tight the living quarters were," Brion said. "But Michelle's girls really took to their new stepfather. They became comfortable enough to call him 'Dad'."

Britt wanted a bigger home and decided to build a large home with the help of his father. The men paid for contractors to pour concrete and establish the foundation, but father and son built the majority of the house by hand.

"People didn't know where the couple were getting the money to build the house," Brion said. "But Britt did most of the work himself after the foundation was laid. So he was able to save a lot of money when it came to sweat equity. That's a testimony to how badly he wanted the marriage between he and Michelle to work out."

When all was said and done, Britt and Michelle Hall were the proud owners of a beautiful 4100 square foot home on ten acres, the perfect place to spend the rest of their lives together. The brand new house boasted vaulted ceilings, granite counter tops, and a finished basement. The construction would prove to be a house of cards, however, as things were brewing underneath the surface.

Michelle didn't have much luck with her two previous marriages, and although individual accounts may vary, her two former husbands are both to have reported being abused by Michelle during the course of their marriage.

Michelle never had a firm grasp on her emotions and didn't handle anger well. These character flaws would not bode well for her life with

Britt. Dealing with both partners' ex-spousal issues including custody and visitation, Michelle and Britt found themselves tinkering on the edge of divorce after a few months into their marriage.

"The way Britt and Michelle handled their issues were different," said family friend Sue Mathis. "Michelle was quicker to speak her mind and a lot of times, Britt just wanted her to try to gain a little bit more self-control."

Dealing with his own ex-wife and their similar divorce problems, Britt Hall was also facing his own internal battles with depression. Although he wasn't often the instigator in their frequent arguments, he was known to fervently engage in the verbal conflicts. While this certainly wasn't conducive to a happy and fruitful marriage, Britt Hall made it clear to friends he would not give up on his family and the life he had built.

The next couple of years came with continued stress, intensified by financial worries after the Halls realized they had gotten too far deep in debt as a result of building their dream home. Notices of foreclosure, liens on the house, and over-extensions were haunting the couple and causing both spouses to hit a breaking point.

On July 30, 2008, it was another typical tense day in the Hall household. Friends say Britt Hall, already aggravated due to a landscaper failing to complete a job on time, went to the store to pick-up hot dogs for a family get-together.

"Hey hon," Britt said as he called his wife. "How many hot dogs do you think I should get-"

"Count how many damn people are here," Michelle snapped. "That's how much you should get."

This would be the snide comeback that would break the straw in Britt's back. He grew tired at her constant bickering and baiting. When he came home that evening, a fight would ensue.

Michelle's youngest daughter, Alyssa, was in the living room watching television as her mother vacuumed to prepare for the company soon arriving. When Britt Hall told Alyssa to turn the TV down, another argument between the couple ensued and Hall immediately told her daughter to go upstairs to her bedroom and not come out until she was called.

There are only two individuals who know the details of what followed on that evening, and only one of them lived to tell. When all was said and done, Britt would be dead and Michelle would be charged with murder.

The 911 call came in at 8:02 p.m. by a frantic Michelle who told dispatchers that her husband had tried to kill her and commit suicide.

"He shot at me, and we were fighting to get it," Michelle told dispatchers regarding the weapon. She said she heard the gun go off twice. Seconds later, she told dispatchers her husband was turning blue.

When police arrived, Britt Hall was dead and had three noticeable gunshot wounds to his body: one on his left arm, one on his right thigh, and a close-range shot to his chest. Michelle Hall, bruised, scraped and covered in blood, told first responders the same story she had told dispatchers: her suicidal husband had tried to kill her before turning the gun on himself.

Prior to further investigation, deputies on the scene immediately called Britt Hall's parents and told them their son had committed suicide. The Halls refused to believe the news.

"Things just seemed to be going too good at this time in his life for him to have done that," said his mother, Charlene Hall. "I knew he didn't kill himself; I knew for a fact that didn't happen."

It didn't take long for police to begin seeing the crime scene a little differently than Michelle had described. Blood splatter and numerous bullet holes covered the downstairs bedroom, and a trail of blood led into the bathroom where Britt Hall's lifeless body now lay. If this was a suicide, there sure was a struggle beforehand.

Investigators gave Michelle the opportunity to explain the scene. She told how an argument between the couple turned violent when

Britt Hall threw her onto the bed. He immediately went into the study and she followed him.

Then she noticed the gun on the computer desk.

Knowing her husband was battling depression, she said she immediately became concerned with his safety, worried that he may use the gun to harm himself.

Michelle stated that she instinctively dove for the gun, and that's when Britt Hall reached for it as well and the two began struggling for possession.

After both Michelle and her husband lost control of he gun, she quickly picked up the weapon and began shooting rounds into the walls and floor in an effort to unload the gun.

In the hall, Britt Hall caught up with her and that's when she said he threatened to kill her. In yet another entanglement of an attempt for control of the gun, Michelle said the gun accidentally went off. This shot punctured Britt Hall's thigh, and that's when Hall claimed she went to call for help.

Britt Hall began crawling into the bathroom, unable to walk and calling out her name for help. When she approached him, gun in hand, she said he grabbed the pistol from her, put it to his chest, and pulled the trigger.

The problem with her story, however, was that most suicides don't entail multiple gunshot wounds. Additionally, the manner in which the fatal shot was delivered raised eyebrows for investigators.

"I've worked many suicides in my career, and I've never worked a suicide that I can remember where a man had shot himself in the chest," Lt John Lewis said.

Furthermore, the gunshot wound on Britt Hall's chest had no signs of charring or burning around the entry wound, signs which usually indicate a self-inflicted wound.

Britt Hall also had a shattered elbow and a bullet hole in his left arm. Three different shots, all which led investigators to believe they weren't being told the whole story.

Michelle did her best to persuade the investigative team to believe her story, but her story changed upon being brought to the station for questioning. While at first she claimed the two struggled for control over the gun, she then claimed Britt Hall was never actually in possession of the gun at all.

Coupled with the evidence at the crime scene and her story's inconsistencies, Michelle was charged the next morning with the murder of her husband.

Crucial to the prosecution's case was the testimony of Michelle's youngest daughter, Alyssa, who was in the home during the shooting. Police brought the 8-year-old in for questioning immediately following the incident and she clearly stated she heard her step-father pleading with her mother to "put the gun down," she said. Alyssa would ultimately testify in her mother's trial in 2009.

Facing charges of malice murder and aggravated assault, Michelle vehemently denied killing her husband. She insisted that he died of a self-inflicted gunshot wound after threatening suicide and fighting with her over the .38 caliber revolver.

The fight that evening was par for the course, she said. The two regularly got into verbal and physical altercations, and their marriage was falling apart due to financial stress. They would also constantly fight over ex-spouses, custody and visitation regarding the six children. Although there were no police reports relating to any domestic altercations in the home before, family and friends knew things weren't okay on the home front.

"Britt would spend several nights driving to work calling me and saying 'I don't know what to do.' He would have done everything in his power to save his marriage, even if it was not worth saving. He was terrified of failure," said Mathis.

One of the first fights that turned physical in front of the family was in November 2006, when Britt Hall's eldest daughter came into the room to find Michelle Hall unconscious. Her father quickly ushered her out of the room and told her not to worry about it. The next couple of years only brought more trouble due to the same old problems and Britt's alleged mental illness.

Britt was prescribed three different types of medication for depression at the time of his death, police confirmed.

But the physical evidence did not add up to suicide. Initially, the Georgia Bureau of Investigation estimated the fatal gunshot to have been fired from around 18-24 inches away. This is not consistent with suicide, detectives argued. While many victims of mental illness fall prey to suicide each year, the facts must add up. In this case, they did not.

If convicted, Michelle was facing life in prison.

In September of 2009, testimonies were heard by Alyssa Davis, as well as responding officers Capt. Tony Grant and Sgt. Freddy Cox, about what they saw and heard on the night of the shooting.

Cox testified that Hall's appearance was "consistent with someone who'd been in a physical altercation" and that Hall had bruises, scrapes and blood on her neck and forehead as well as blood on her hands and a knot on her elbow.

During his testimony, Grant stated he immediately noticed that Hall's face was red and she had what appeared to be gun-shot residue on her hand, even though she was stating her husband had committed suicide.

There were multiple bullet holes throughout the downstairs of the home when police arrived on the scene, Grant testified. Two bullets were recovered from Britt Hall's body and three more were found in the house.

Grant said a blood pattern analysis showed blood spatters of 90 degrees in the downstairs quarters outside of the bathroom, proof that Britt Hall crawled into the bathroom after being wounded.

Defense Attorney Mike Kam said that while in no uncertain terms would he call the key ear witness a liar, her age and her location during the shooting did not make for the most reliable testimony.

"She was eight; she didn't see anything, she clearly got some of the facts confused." Kam said in an interview. "She's not someone who is used to being asked questions in formal interview settings. Who knows what she remembered, or what happened?"

Additionally, Kam indicated that Michelle certainly didn't fit the description of a murderer. Outside of two divorces, Hall had no criminal record. She was law-abiding citizen, with nothing in her background which would give the assumption she was capable of murder, he said.

But the jury had heard enough. On September 25, 2009, Michelle Hall was found guilty on all counts in the death of her husband Britt.

Not long after her conviction, Hall's attorneys filed a motion for a new trial, citing trial court errors. Coweta County Superior Court Judge Jack Kirby denied the motion and the defense attorneys took the case to the Supreme Court.

On September 22, 2010, the Supreme Court of Georgia upheld the conviction, despite Hall's defense's argument that the trial court erred by admitting similar transaction evidence and prior consistent statements.

Hall's defense stated that testimony from both of her ex-husbands that she was verbally and physically abusive were inadmissible because they were not "sufficiently similar" to establish proof of the crimes for which she was charged, according to the opinion of the Supreme Court. It also stated that "in cases of domestic violence, prior incidents of abuse against family members or sexual partners are more generally permitted because there is a logical connection between violent acts against two different persons with whom the accused had a similar emotional or intimate attachment."

The opinion also added that the fifteen and thirteen-year lapses of time between her ex-husband's allegations of abuse to the alleged shooting of her husband did not require exclusion of evidence.

"Given that the similar transaction evidence reflects appellant's behavior towards prior spouses, we conclude that any prejudice from the age of these prior incidents was outweighed by the probative value of the evidence under the particular facts of this case and the purpose for which the similar transactions were offered."

Eighteen months later, however, Michelle retained a new attorney who filed a habeas corpus petition, stating Michelle was given ineffective legal counsel by Kam during her trial in 2009. Senior Judge Robert B. Struble presided over the hearing and determined that Hall was in-fact entitled to a new trial. Struble agreed that Kam, Hall's trial attorney, was "ineffective and fell below the minimum guarantee of representation under the constitution," a press release said.

While Michelle may have been looking forward to another chance at redemption, The Attorney General's Office quickly announced their plans to appeal the habeas corpus ruling to the Georgia Supreme Court.

In a press release on March 30, 2012, Coweta County District Attorney Peter John Skandalakis expressed his respectful disapproval of the court's ruling and that in stating Kam was ineffective for representation, "the court erroneously applied the wrong standard under the law."

Skandalakis said he was optimistic that the Supreme Court will conclude that Hall had a legally sufficient defense and that her conviction would be upheld after review of the appeal.

On January 22, 2013, the Supreme Court found Hall's convictions to be fair and just, denying insufficient representation during her 2009 trial. According to the court summary, the Supreme Court concluded that the habeas corpus petition did not conduct proper legal analysis to determine the effectiveness of Hall's defense.

The opinion references Strickland v. Washington, a 1984 Supreme Court case in which it determined that to be granted a new trial, a defendant must show that it was due to insufficient performance by defense that the defendant was found guilty.

Michelle's argument for her habeas corpus petition was that "if she were in the same room when her young daughter was questioned, she could have assisted her attorney by prompting him with specific information," the court says in its opinion. However, it was determined during the habeas hearing that any information she would have portrayed to her attorney was already known information to both parties. "As such, Hall has failed to show actual prejudice, and her claim of ineffective assistance of counsel should have been rejected," the opinion said.

Today, Michelle Hall remains in a Coweta County prison.

Since her conviction, Michelle's ex-husbands have been given full custody of her three respective daughters.

She won't be eligible for parole until 2039. She will be 70 years old.

www.ingramcontent.com/pod-product-compliance
Lightning Source LLC
Chambersburg PA
CBHW021955170726
47994CB00021B/426